RELIGION AND SOCIETY

ESSAYS ON THE PHILOSOPHICAL NEXUS BETWEEN RELIGION AND POLITICS

VOLUME 2

RELIGION AND SOCIETY

Additional books in this series can be found on Nova's website under the Series tab.

Additional e-books in this series can be found on Nova's website under the eBooks tab.

RELIGION AND SOCIETY

ESSAYS ON THE PHILOSOPHICAL NEXUS BETWEEN RELIGION AND POLITICS

VOLUME 2

EMANUEL L. PAPARELLA

Copyright © 2018 by Nova Science Publishers, Inc.

All rights reserved. No part of this book may be reproduced, stored in a retrieval system or transmitted in any form or by any means: electronic, electrostatic, magnetic, tape, mechanical photocopying, recording or otherwise without the written permission of the Publisher.

We have partnered with Copyright Clearance Center to make it easy for you to obtain permissions to reuse content from this publication. Simply navigate to this publication's page on Nova's website and locate the "Get Permission" button below the title description. This button is linked directly to the title's permission page on copyright.com. Alternatively, you can visit copyright.com and search by title, ISBN, or ISSN.

For further questions about using the service on copyright.com, please contact:
Copyright Clearance Center
Phone: +1-(978) 750-8400   Fax: +1-(978) 750-4470   E-mail: info@copyright.com.

NOTICE TO THE READER

The Publisher has taken reasonable care in the preparation of this book, but makes no expressed or implied warranty of any kind and assumes no responsibility for any errors or omissions. No liability is assumed for incidental or consequential damages in connection with or arising out of information contained in this book. The Publisher shall not be liable for any special, consequential, or exemplary damages resulting, in whole or in part, from the readers' use of, or reliance upon, this material. Any parts of this book based on government reports are so indicated and copyright is claimed for those parts to the extent applicable to compilations of such works.

Independent verification should be sought for any data, advice or recommendations contained in this book. In addition, no responsibility is assumed by the publisher for any injury and/or damage to persons or property arising from any methods, products, instructions, ideas or otherwise contained in this publication.

This publication is designed to provide accurate and authoritative information with regard to the subject matter covered herein. It is sold with the clear understanding that the Publisher is not engaged in rendering legal or any other professional services. If legal or any other expert assistance is required, the services of a competent person should be sought. FROM A DECLARATION OF PARTICIPANTS JOINTLY ADOPTED BY A COMMITTEE OF THE AMERICAN BAR ASSOCIATION AND A COMMITTEE OF PUBLISHERS.

Additional color graphics may be available in the e-book version of this book.

Library of Congress Cataloging-in-Publication Data

ISBN: 978-1-53613-135-2

Published by Nova Science Publishers, Inc. † New York

"True to form, my fellow Yale alumnus Dr. Emanuel L. Paparella has once again come out with a brilliant book of essays. This one deals with the thorny but perennial theme of the interface between Religion and Politics, two human phenomena which have had a love-hate relationship from time immemorial within the history of civilizations. Indeed, the nexus religion-politics has constituted a passionate scholarly concern of his for several decades. It appears not only in his Ph.D. dissertation on the Concept of Providence within the philosophy of history of Giambattista Vico, presented in the late 80s at Yale University, but in just about all of his extraordinary books within the field of cultural anthropology. Dr. Paparella has been reflecting long and hard on this thorny subject. This book will delight readers interested in the history and development of civilizations. It is replete with original insights and is nothing short than the distillation of years of reflections on the subject. Those reflections will prove essential to any contemporary attempt at rescuing our troubled Western civilization which Dr. Paparella describes as a civilization in search of its soul.

--Dr. Michael Vena, Professor Emeritus,
Southern Connecticut State University

"Emanuel L. Paparella has for many years researched the hot theme of the nexus between religion and politics, or religion and democracy. He has done so on a purely theoretical level but also on an historical level, thus exploring a vast field of knowledge. He possesses a consummate ability to relate to each other different cultural traditions from which he is able to derive original points of reflection. The theme of the nexus religion and politics, given our current philosophical confusion on fundamental values, is, in my opinion,

central for the construction of a society which remains free and just, as professor Paparella certainly augurs."

--Professor Ernesto Paolozzi,
Philosophy Professor,
University of Suor Orsola Benincasa, Naples, Italy

"Dr. Paparella's choice of subjects is wide and varied, reflecting on problems both old and new, and makes for engaging, thought provoking reading. Though it has been said there is nothing new under the sun, reading Dr. Paparella's work gives one a new understanding and appreciation for the great philosophers through the ages, and an invigorating direction for the future."

--Professor Michael Newman,
Broward College, Davie, FL

Democracy is not a political concept but it is a way of life. It is a fundamental axiom of a healthy society. The conversation between life and democracy is a constant process and includes the nexus between democracy and religion. Professor Paparella's essays on the nexus between Democracy and Religion, masterfully unveil the truths in this nexus, without avoiding ideological, theoretical or political conflicts. They search in depth, under the surface of contemporary practices and events, for true relationships and communications between religion, democracy and a healthy society.

--Thanos Kalamidas, Chief Editor
Ovi magazine and Ovi project

CONTENTS

Volume 2

Preface		ix
Essay 1	Is Northern Europe Still the Last Bastion of Liberal Tolerance?	1
Essay 2	Irshad Manji on Faith, Freedom, Human Rights and Love: Why Opposing Religion via a Politico-Secular Discourse is a Blunder	7
Essay 3	Some Distinctions on Christian and Secular Humanism	13
Essay 4	An Imaginary Conversation on Myth, Reason and Religion between Plato and Joseph Campbell at an Athens Café	23
Essay 5	The Immigrant "Other" in US and EU Politico-Religious Experiences: A Comparative Perspective	37
Essay 6	Eight Scholars' Views (Dante, Husserl, Levinas, Dawson, Weiler, Habermas, Eisenstadt and Troeltsch) on the Loss of European Spiritual Identity	49

Essay 7	The Corruption of Religion: Russia's Military-Ecclesiastical Complex	93
Essay 8	Corruption and the Self-Destruction of Democracy	101
Essay 9	Pope Francis's Urgent Warning on the Dangers of Populism	105
Essay 10	White Supremacy in the White House: Rooted in a Dark Theory of History	109
Essay 11	Power without Moral Compass: Caligula, Trump, Pius XIII, and Machiavelli	117
Essay 12	Honor, Ethics, Shame, Guilt and Civilization	123
Essay 13	A New World Order: The End of Pax Americana and Putin's Enigmatic New Russianness	129
Essay 14	Democracy: The Missing Ingredient in the Bannon/Dugin Concept of Eurasianism	135
Essay 15	The Stubborn Facts on Eurocentrism: Nostalgia for the Cold War, Misinformation, and the Russian National Identity Discourse	145
Essay 16	The Nightmare of Modern Democracy in the Age of Alternate Facts: A Sickness unto Death?	153
Essay 17	Pope Francis's Critique of Bannon's Views on Christianity	159
Essay 18	Darkness at Twilight: The Devil's Bargain in American Politics?	163

About the Author 167

Index 169

PREFACE

This book contains 18 essays of various lengths written over a three year span (2015-2017) on the theme of the historical nexus between democracy or, more generally speaking, politics and religion, the sacred and the secular.

The book casts a sweeping cultural view on a theme related to the following philosophical dialectical phenomena: mythological/historical, poetical/scientific, political/transcendent, freedom/determinism, ideological/historical, raw power/justice, law/love, grand-narrative /positivistic approach, tradition/modernity, transcendence/immanence, secular/religious, liberal/fascist, freedom/necessity, freedom/rights, freedom/determinism, democratic ideals/political corruption, moral compass/real politick, guilt/honor, Machiavellism/transparency, universally valid ethical tradition/historical relativistic ethical tradition, utilitalian approach/deontological approach, secular humanism/religious humanism, public/private spirituality, spiritual/political identity.

These subthemes are alluded to in the very title of each essay and then philosophically explored. They venture into uncharted territory, challenging conventional geo-political assumptions about history, progress, science, the secular and the sacred. The goal is not so much to solve those perennial conundrums of the human condition, but to point to their relevancy for getting some effective handle on our varied contemporary existential predicaments in politics, in environmental science and in spirituality. For example a problematic extensively explored throughout the book is this: are the great religious traditions universal and open to everybody, or are they connected to particular ethnic people and civilizations? Another is this: how does the separation of Church from State, of temporal power from spiritual power, constitute a thorny cultural problem from the very beginning of Western Civilization, or for that matter, of any kind of civilization? Still another is the often unperceived distinction between secular and religious humanism. Most educated people know that it began in Italy in the 14th century but imagine it as an anti-religion movement. It is far from that.

One essay that perhaps best represents the core ideas, the very essence of this thematic collection is essay 24 titled "Eight Scholars' Views (Dante, Husserl, Levinas, Dawson, Weiler, Habermas, Eisenstadt and Troeltsch) on the Loss of the European Spiritual Identity."

The target audience, as the publishers suggest in their advertisement of the book, includes those educated persons interested in education, in the history of ideas, in philosophy and history' s development, in the liberal arts, in the philosophy of history, while remaining concerned with the time-old particular nexus between democracy and religion. More inclusively, a complete education means that one remains aware of the importance of pursuing the complex and often thorny nexus between religion and politics, a philosophical phenomenon predating democracy itself and existing since the birth of the polis. The essays are also sure to appeal to those visionary scholars seeking not only the origins of the philosophy of history, but all that is true, beautiful and good in the world, those who follow contemporary developments in ethics and spirituality.

Finally, I'd like to announce that this book is dedicated to my lovely wife Cathy, my three daughters Cristina, Alessandra, and Francesca, as well as my four beloved grandchildren: Sophia, Nicholas, Adrianna, and Collin. In various ways they have complemented the more theoretical aspects of the search for truth, by assisting me with the more practical aspects of its preparation and being a source of encouragement and inspiration. I trust that eventually it will become part of their intellectual heritage.

Emanuel L. Paparella, Ph.D.
Lake Worth, Palm Beach County, FL
October 2017

Essay 1

IS NORTHERN EUROPE STILL THE LAST BASTION OF LIBERAL TOLERANCE?

Figure 1.1. Flags of the EU.

I grew up thinking of the Scandinavian and Northern European countries (Sweden, Denmark, the Netherland, etc.) as the most liberal societies in Europe, the very bastion of tolerance, enlightenment and democracy. Is that still the case today? Considering the latest reports from these countries on the steady increase of populist anti-Islamic forces one is left wondering.

The words "democracy" and "cultural tolerance," and "multiculturalism" are still given lip service in those societies, but the sad reality is that those countries far from being the bastion of liberalism and tolerance, seem to be getting perilously accommodating to the claims of radical-right parties of the EU. Consider the entry of the Sweden Democrats, so called, into the Swedish parliament after the elections of September 2010, or the Danish People's Party of Pia Kjaesgaard which supports right-wing minority governments since 2001, while the Party for Freedom (PVV) of Geert Wilders is practically playing a similar role in the Netherlands. This kind of news is quite disconcerting for liberals in general who are known for their advocacy of cultural tolerance and harmony.

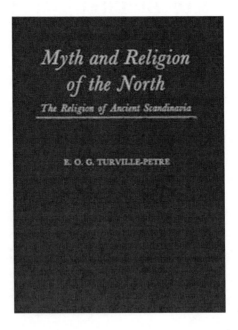

Figure 1.2. Is the North of Europe the seat of the EU culture?

A closer look into European citizens' political attitudes needs to be taken. Then one discovers a more complex but more reassuring picture. It shows that the Northern countries remain among the most culturally tolerant countries worldwide. For example a relatively recent poll found that while some 14% of EU citizens can be classified as "intolerant," only 11% in the Netherlands and 9% in Sweden could be so classified. Surprisingly, Denmark topped them all with 20%. Sweden scored as 76% tolerant against a EU average of merely 60%, while Denmark, once again, scored lower with 64%. This of course does not mean that things have been improving, if anything, they have been getting worse in the area of cultural tolerance.

For example, a 2005 May Pew survey rated the Dutch as among the most anti-Muslim among Europeans. They have been singled out the Dutch, and to a less extend the Danish, as tolerant of Islamophobia by the European Monitoring Center on Racism and Xenophobia (EUMC) and the European Commission against Racism and Intolerance (ECRI).

How does one explain this conundrum? Could it be that it is precisely their former extreme tolerance that permits the present intolerance? To answer that question one needs to look at two other crucial elements besides tolerance itself: nationalism and conformism.

It is a fact that in the countries under discussion tolerance has always been associated with a negative attitude toward ethnic chauvinistic nationalism. They considered themselves "non-nationalist nations" which sounds like an oxymoron but it makes sense if one thinks what extreme nationalism has wrought to Europe. Nationalism was linked to Nazism and the extreme radical right-wing parties. Hence the option of relating anti-immigrant and Xenophobic policies to a nationalistic narrative (as was the case in Austria, Belgium or France) never existed in Denmark, the Netherlands or Sweden.

Moreover, there is conformity at play; a well-known component of the Northern European ethos. It is used frequently by their politician as a weapon to enforce political correctness. There is in these countries a high trust in state actors and institutions. There was a certain image of the Nordic people to be kept in good standing, that of a people in genuine love with multiculturalism, cultural tolerance, liberalism with a vengeance. Thus the immigration issue was kept off the agenda for a while.

Figure 1.3. Ansgar who converted the Swedes to Christianity.

What is also intriguing in this analysis is that while those countries remain among the most tolerant on women's rights, gay rights, they are also among the EU least religious societies and the most secular; religion seems to be treated as just another myth comparable to the ancient Nordic myth; which seems to bolster the misguided argument that religion should not be included in the public agora of any enlightened society, but also reveals a vulnerability: religion having been marginalized, it has also been politicized and reduced to the level of another political ideology and propaganda. In this context, it is quite easy to interpret Islam as a threat to European culture and to liberal democracy.

For the moment we can say here that, to the chagrin of the Islamophobes and Xenophobes and the religiously challenged of the EU, Islam remains a growing religion that understandably threatens the secularist consensus of the EU by bringing religious issues back onto the public agenda. Of course the threat is perceived to be not only to secularism but also to gender equality, gay rights, liberal democracy; all considered fundamental aspects of Western Civilization.

Figure 1.4. Does religion-less spell political tolerance?

Hence, so the argument goes, it is incumbent for all tolerant Europeans, (who however are loath to acknowledge that inalienable human rights have a religious origin in Christianity; an acknowledgement which could counter the intolerances of Islam in those areas), to oppose the "intolerant" Muslims. Now, that may or may not explain the paradox of intolerance in the most liberal countries of the EU but it remains a clever by half stratagem; that is to say, the stratagem of opposing orthodox Islam with a liberal-democratic discourse rather than a more boorish ethnic-nationalistic conformist one. The stratagem works to a certain extent: it makes it politically acceptable to many misguided people in those countries under the delusion that religion is just another myth to be disposed of and that secularism will ultimately triumph. Those people have utterly failed to read and ponder Jorge's Habermas' essay on "A post-secular Europe." They ought to do so at their earliest convenience or be utterly disappointed by future events in Sweden, Denmark and the Netherland, not to speak of the whole EU.

Essay 2

IRSHAD MANJI ON FAITH, FREEDOM, HUMAN RIGHTS AND LOVE:
WHY OPPOSING RELIGION VIA A POLITICO-SECULAR DISCOURSE IS A BLUNDER

Figure 2.1. Does politico-secular discourse lead to Sharia?

As regards the attitude of liberal societies toward religious belief, we have so far argued that the stratagem of opposing intolerant social norms as practices by some Muslim communities vis a vis women, gays, human rights and freedom in general (be it of speech, or political, or artistic); that is to say, opposing certain religiously condoned intolerances and orthodoxies with a libertarian "enlightened" secular discourse (which usually advocates the liquidation of religion per se, at best tolerating a mere vapid cafeteria-style sort of "spirituality") is an inadequate, merely clever by half, solution to the problem at hand. It makes those who feel that their faith is under attack all the more determined to defend it zealously. In Islam they call that kind of extreme defense Jihad and it has been carried in one form or another for centuries now.

What usually happens is that the table adroitly gets turned around and the "enlightened" "progressive" secularist alleging human rights violations that need to be abolished ends up getting himself accused of intolerance, of trying to impose his particular brand of intolerance, i.e., his secularism, on believers. This is particularly true in societies where religion has been abandoned as just another myth or lie, long superseded by modernity progressive positivistic science. Not to be modern is to be medieval, obscurantist, retrograde, undesirables who cannot be accommodated in a modern progressive society based on the tenets of the Enlightenment, a la Voltaire.

This approach usually misfires and ends up producing more animosity and intolerance with accusations of zealotry and extremism on both sides of the fence. There is however a much better approach and it is that advocated by the influential philosopher Jurgen Habermas in his essay "A post-secular Europe" and that of the Ugandan born Canadian Muslim Irshad Manji, author of two best-selling influential books: *The Trouble with Islam Today* (translated into 30 languages), and *How to Reconcile Faith and Freedom.*

She has received an honorary degree in the history of ideas from the University of British Columbia, and a governor general medal as a top humanities graduate; initiated the TV project *Moral Courage* with

Professor Cornell West becoming a critic of mainstream Islam, and participated in the TV series *America at a Crossroads* titled "Faith without Fear." Moreover, she has addressed numerous audiences at the UN and at Amnesty International.

Figure 2.2. Is the problem the use or the abuse?

At NYU Wagner, Irshad teaches a course titled "Moral Courage and Your Purpose." Among the professional skills that students can expect to learn: articulating how you want to serve your society, identifying your core values, turning your values into action, knowing when to step up or step back, and staying motivated to deliver on your vision.

Let's take a brief look at her thinking as regards the reforming of Islam. In the first place she points out that she is in no way advocating the abolishing of Islam but its reform, or better, its re-interpretation. The words of the Koran are not to be abolished or rewritten, but what is written gets re-interpreted as it was meant to be all along. What does that mean? That the Torah, the Bible and the Koran need to be interpreted by the mere fact that they contain symbolical language: poetry, parables and stories that need to be constantly interpreted in the light of the existential events of human history in order for them to have any meaningful application for our existential situation. In other words, she is far from advocating a throwing away of the baby (faith) with the dirty water (the corruption within a religion) as many secular humanists end up doing when they suggest that religion does not properly belong in the public agora and ought to be relegated, with other myths, to the dustbin of history.

Figure 2.3. Is liberty based on love?

Manji arrived at this conclusion when she began comparing various religious beliefs after being expelled from the Moslem religious school she was attending as a teenager eight hours a week, for asking too many questions. She found her faith anew by leaving her faith for a while and freely researching other faiths. For example she discovered that the image many Muslims, Jews and Christians have of God was that of a vengeful law-giver bent on enforcing the law with a vengeance. That is not her interpretation of who this God really is as per Holy Scriptures. He seems to her to be benevolent and merciful, not nasty and brutish, more in the image of man. Since this God created all there is, or had a plan for all creatures, not excluding Lesbians and Gays, it remains to be explained how he can then act against the logic of his own creation.

To recapitulate the above discourse with what was analyzed in the previous essay regarding the paradox of Scandinavian progressive anti-nationalistic, liberal societies slowly beginning to tolerate Islamophobia and Xenophobia, perhaps it would be a much wiser strategy on their part to identify the intolerances and abuses of human rights found in religions such as Islam and Christianity and Judaism, not in the religion per se but in its misinterpretations, and advocate their reform rather than their liquidation. One can wager that most reasonable Muslims would be willing to listen to the voice of a reasoned discourse that does not include the liquidation of religion and a vapid substitution with "spirituality" disrespectful of the tradition and the cultural heritage of a particular religion. Irshad Manji offers us a great example on how this can be accomplished.

In conclusion, as that wise man in Palestine who started a new religion in the Middle East which then came to Rome and Athens and ended up becoming perhaps the best component of Europe's cultural identity after the fall of the Roman Empire, used to quip: "let those who have ears, let them hear."

Essay 3

SOME DISTINCTIONS ON CHRISTIAN AND SECULAR HUMANISM

Figure 3.1. Where are the origins of Christian Humanism?

Francesco Petrarca (14th century, father of Humanism), G. K. Chesterton, Christopher Dawson, T. S. Eliot, Desiderius Erasmus, Thomas More, Francis of Assisi, Pope Francis, Christopher Fry, Immanuel Kant, Soren Kierkegaard, Blaise Pascal, Martin Luther King Jr., Gabriel Marcel Jacques Maritain, Thomas Merton, Emmanuel Mounier, John Henry Newman, Reinhold Niebuhr, Charles Peguy, Dorothy Day, Paul Tillich.

What is the one thing that all these disparate luminaries have in common? They are all Christian Humanists. The modern secular humanists, however, consider the identification of "Christian Humanist" an oxymoron of sorts. They see the slogan of Anaxagoras that "man is the measure of all things" as confirming their belief that humanism and religion are mutually exclusive. I submit that, to the contrary, they are complementary, that they can be synthesized and rather than an oxymoron they ought to be considered a paradox. How so?

Figure 3.2. Francesco Petrarca.

In the first place Christianity is the only religion (not a mythology, nor a fairy tale) which declares that God became man, took on human nature and dwelt among us; hence it puts emphasis on the humanity of Jesus the Christ, his social teaching and his proclivity to synthesize human spirituality and materialism. It regards universal human dignity and brotherhood, and freedom, and the primacy of human happiness as quite compatible with the teachings of Jesus. In fact Christian humanism can be interpreted as a philosophical union of Christian ethics and humanistic principles. The father of modern humanism, after all, Francesco Petrarca was a deacon of the Church.

Figure 3.3. St. Augustine.

But the roots of Christian humanism go further back to the Jewish concept of humans made in the image of God and Christian theologians such as Justin Martyr (*The Apology*) discovered great value in classical culture, as also did Augustine or the Cappadocian Fathers (Basil of Caesarea and Gregory of Nyssa; which is at the basis of the appreciation of personal dignity, individual worth, social justice, righteousness, and inalienable rights. The great Renaissance Platonist Marsilio Ficino who wrote "On the dignity of man," or even Thomas Jefferson did not invent those concepts out of nothing; they gathered them from a Christian tradition which unfortunately was more often than not paid lip service to, but breached in practice, despite the fancy designation of "enlightened modern ideas."

Figure 3.4. Monks preserving Western Civilization.

After the fall of the Roman Empire Western Christian clerics controlled education, since only the monasteries remained as seats of learning preserving ancient manuscripts and the remnants of Greco-Roman civilization and in part preparing the Renaissance. Charlemagne requested that scholars set up places of learning that would become universities in the 12th century; the first one opened in Bologna in 1088. Eastern Christians meanwhile continued the late Antique practice of studying in the homes of secular masters, studying the same curriculum of classical Greek authors as their predecessors in the Roman period: Homer's Iliad, Plato's dialogues, Aristotle's Categories, Demosthenes' speeches, Galen, Dioscurides, Strabo, and others. Christian education in the East largely was relegated to learning to read the Bible at the knees of one's parents and the rudiments of grammar in the letters of Basil or the homilies of Gregory Nazianzus.

Some Distinctions on Christian and Secular Humanism 17

Abelard in the 11th century attempted to apply formal aspects of Greek philosophy, namely syllogistic reasoning, to inform the process of theology. Western universities including Padua, Bologna, Paris, and Oxford resulted from the so-called Gregorian Reform, which encouraged a new kind of cleric clustered around cathedrals, the so called secular canon. The cathedral schools meant to train clerics for the growing clerical bureaucracy soon served as training grounds for talented young men to train in medicine, law, and the liberal arts of the quadrivium and trivium, in addition to Christian theology. Classical Latin texts and translations of Greek texts served as the basis of non-theological education. A primitive humanism way before the century of humanism (the 13th century, the age of Petrarch, Boccaccio and Dante) actually started when the papacy began protecting the Northern Cluniacs and Cistercians and the Church formed a unifying bond. St. Bernard counseled kings. Priests were frequently Lord Chancellors in England and in France. Christian views became present in all aspects of society, and there was an emphasis on serving God and others. Furthermore, there was a view of human nature that was both hopeful and Christian. All offices, including civil ones, and academic works had religious elements. In addition, religion influenced medicine with the Good Samaritan of the Gospel of Luke. The idea of free people under God came from this time and spread from the West to other areas of the world.

Figure 3.5. Is Christian Humanism tied to Christian ethics?

The explosion of Christian humanism happened in the 15th century with the arrival of the Renaissance, emanating from an increased faith in the abilities of Man, married with a still-firm devotion to Christianity, Petrarch(1304–1374) being considered the father of humanism, one of the earliest and most prominent Renaissance figures. In his letter "The Ascent of Mt. Ventoux" he states that his climb of the mountain was inspired by Livy, but found its true meaning in St. Augustine's Confessions. Here is a synthesis of the classical with the Christian which became the hallmark of the subsequent two centuries of the Renaissance (15th and 16th century). His masterful contributions to language and literature triggered the development of studia humanitas which began to formalize the study of ancient languages, namely Greek and Latin, eloquence, classical authors, and rhetoric. Christian humanists also cared about scriptural and patristic writings, Hebrew, ecclesiastical reform, clerical education, and preaching. A Botticelli or a Michelangelo are incomprehensible without considering this synthesis of the Greco-Roman and the Judeo-Christian which gave a cultural identity to Europe. The Reformation followed carried on by the Catholic Erasmus, the Lutheran Martin Luther (a former Augustinian priest) and John Calvin who studied Scriptures in their original languages (Hebrew, Greek and Latin. That too was in the tradition of Christian Humanism.

It was The Enlightenment of the 18th century that began the separation of religious and secular institutions, to a false rift between Christianity and Humanism. Enter the Deists or rationalists who rejected traditional theology in favor of 'natural religion'. They sidestep the churches and seek God personally by way of reason and innate moral intuition. A scholarly quest for the historical Jesus to fit him within the precepts of bourgeois liberalism. They gave new currency to Christ's humanist ethics and spawned a wave of social gospel liberalism in the 20th century. They effectively reasserted the Judeo-Christian ethic which would play an important role in animating the political and social reform movements of the 19th and 20th centuries. Perhaps the most valuable contribution of this liberal Christianity is that it gave rise to the first British movement for the abolition of slavery, which was founded by the Quakers in the late 18th

Some Distinctions on Christian and Secular Humanism   19

century. However, it was the Evangelical Christian humanism of William Wilberforce (24 August 1759 – 29 July 1833) that led to the successful abolition of the slave trade.

Figure 3.6. Has the Enlightenment still to enlighten itself?

Closer to our times, after the carnage of World War I shattered liberal optimism and the boundless optimism of the secularist Enlightenment is eclipsed by the dark side of humanity and this prompted a realist backlash amongst Christian scholars and theologians such as Niebhur and Barth. Both were erstwhile political liberals but they now insisted on getting back to 'basics'. The curse of original sin seemed borne out by the horrors of the war and any humanist aspirations would now have to be rooted in a theology of redemption and acceptance of complete human dependence on God. They were called "neo-orthodox." But by the 1970s a strident social Christianity had re-emerged. Taking root in the fertile soil of rampant injustice in Latin America and the anti-apartheid struggles in South Africa,

Liberation Theology' aimed at harnessing Christianity to the cause of social justice and even revolutionary socialism. However the title itself was misleading as it was never really a 'theology'. The legacy of social gospel humanism has been carried forward by notables such as Bonhoeffer, Sayers, Williams, O'Connor, Dawson, Solzhenitsyn.

Since the advent of postmodernism, some radical 'progressive' "secularist" "enlightened" Christians have tended to see the Christ of faith as irreconcilable with the Jesus of history, regarding the latter as a mere mortal and a distinctly fallible one at that. Others have made him a mere mythological figure who never existed historically. Since this myth originated in the Middle East it is seen as foreign to the original European culture based on mythological figures such as Zeus, Odin or Thor. They argue for a religion-less non-theistic form of Christianity: the so called Secular Humanist Religion and Ethics for the 21st century. In practice they have substituted the religion of Christ with the religion of soccer games. Since we all go to soccer games we are all Europeans. They take a deconstructionist view that dogmatic theology is suspect and spiritual truth is mainly a personalized and subjective pursuit.

Figure 3.7. Christopher Dawson, author of *The Making of Europe*.

There have been various attempts to reclaim a more traditional Christian humanism and reclaim Christianity's rich cultural heritage but so far the omens are not good. This Christian humanism emphasizes Jesus as the incarnate fusing of humanity with the divine—humanity in the image of God—especially as manifested in the sublime, creative achievements of Western civilization. These ideas had previously reached their peak in the Renaissance and the Renaissance humanists that supported the Catholic Church, such as Erasmus, Thomas More, Johann Reuchlin, John Colet and the others above mentioned. So far the religion of soccer games is winning and the Church has been declared dead. But she has an uncanny way of returning to life. Hope springs anew.

Essay 4

AN IMAGINARY CONVERSATION ON MYTH, REASON AND RELIGION BETWEEN PLATO AND JOSEPH CAMPBELL AT AN ATHENS CAFÉ

"According to Greek mythology, humans were originally created with four arms, four legs and a head with two faces. Fearing their power, Zeus split them into two separate parts, condemning them to spend their lives in search of their other halves."

— *Plato,* The Symposium

"Life is like arriving late for a movie, having to figure out what was going on without bothering everybody with a lot of questions, and then being unexpectedly called away before you find out how it ends."

— *Joseph Campbell,* Creative Mythology

Figure 4.1. Plato.

Figure 4.2. Joseph Campbell.

An Imaginary Conversation on Myth, Reason and Religion ...

Author's Preface: What follows is a spirited, imaginary, rather mundane conversation across time, between a well-known ancient philosopher and a well-known modern mythologist at a café in Athens overlooking the acropolis. While the conversation is purely imaginary, not overly academic, and rather colloquial at that, the integrity of the thought of its interlocutors on myth, reason and religion within the existential historical circumstances of both men has been scrupulously adhered to, and respected, for not to do so would be to fall into sophistry of the worst kind.

Figure 4.3. The Acropolis as seen from a cafè in Athens.

Plato: Good morning Professor Campbell!

Campbell: Good morning Professor Plato! I trust you don't mind such a title, even though you are so famous that your nick name is enough to identify you. After all, you were the founder- director, the first professor so to speak, of the ancient Greek Academy; an intellectual achievement which thrived for a thousand years.

Plato. Oh, yes, yes, why don't we simply dispense with formal titles? May I just call you Joe and you call me Plato? After all, we are not at a formal symposium or at an academic conference; we're just sipping cognac and chatting at a café in modern Athens in view of the acropolis.

Campbell. By all means, Plato. In America, in fact, we prefer to dispense with too many formalities and pomposity. Perhaps later we may even engage in a chess game and a pipe smoke, should you have the time. Those are pastimes suitable to reflective minds. I can teach you, if you are unfamiliar with them.

Plato. Sounds like a good idea, Joe. That way, while we may be discussing transcendent ideas beyond time and space, we shall not give the false impression to passerby that we are two of those unpractical philosophers with a beard, with their heads in the clouds of Mount Olympus, exchanging recondite abstract reveries; rather, that we are practical men of the world, clever enough to put theory ahead of practice.

Campbell. Indeed, Plato, indeed. Human nature being what it is, it cannot have been a piece of cake for you to manage the logistics of the administration of a great academy and keep discipline among rowdy students and competing professors and their contemptuous ad hominem antics and juvenile slanderous attacks on each other. I know something about that. I am an insider in the academic where I have sojourned all my life, but in reality, intellectually and spiritually that is, I have always felt like an outsider, a non-conventional academic who did not even bother to finish his Ph.D. dissertation, albeit I am presently widely known as the foremost mythology expert and scholar of the Western world.

Plato. Ah yes, "the Ph.D. octopus"! I have read the essay on the subject by our colleague, your fellow countryman, William James. Excellent insightful essay; an exposé of sorts, it almost made me ashamed of having given rise to the term "academic."

Campbell: Plato, you are justifiably recognized as the one who brought to a head the philosophical conundrums of myth/history, reason/myth, religion/myth; all the more since you yourself repeatedly utilizes mythology and concocted myths in your dialogues and treatises, the best known of course being the myth of the cave as found in your Republic.

An Imaginary Conversation on Myth, Reason and Religion ...

Figure 4.4. Plato's Myth of the Cave in the Republic.

Plato: Quite right Joe, quite right. The Cave, the narrative that occurs in the *Republic* is a fantastical story, but it does not deal explicitly with the beyond, and is thus different from the traditional myths I used and those I invented. Strictly speaking, the Cave is an analogy, not a myth. Also in the *Republic,* Socrates says that until philosophers take control of a city "the politeia whose story we are telling in words (*muthologein*) will not achieve its fulfillment in practice." The construction of the ideal city itself may be called a "myth" in the sense that it depicts an imaginary polis where we imagine the happy state. In the *Phaedrus* I use the word *muthos* to name the rhetorical exercise which Socrates carries out, but this seems to be a loose usage of the word. In any case, when I inveighed against the bad poets I certainly did not have the likes of Homer or his Odyssey or Iliad in mind. I respect and revere the likes of Homer, or Shakespeare or Dante. What I was critiquing was the mind-set of those inferior mediocre poets, the poets who write poems for wedding receptions and then claim to be great poets; those with no poetical vision who couldn't even write a decent novel, never mind an epic poem. Did you know that in my youth I had aspired to be a poet?

Campbell: Yes I know, Plato, and it doesn't surprise me a bit judging from the complex beauty of your ancient Greek prose which depicts your myths so well. But what I am particularly interested in is in finding out why you included myths such as "the myth of the cave" in the Republic?

How did that help your rational philosophical discourse about good governance, democracy, justice? You seem to conceive of myth as a clue to the search for life's meaning. I, on the other hand, see them as a clue to the spiritual potentialities of human life. For me myths are the ongoing search for "the experience of life." They seem to tell us is that the meaning of life *is* the experience of life, that eternity isn't some later time, or a long time; that in fact it has nothing to do with time! It is that dimension of here and now which thinking and time cuts out, but it seems to me that if you don't get it here, you won't get it anywhere; that the experience of eternity right here and now is the function of life.

Plato: Oh well. Frankly, I am a bit surprised that you should even ask such a question as the eminent mythologist that you are. As you well know, mythology as well as drama sprang directly from the realm of the religious and the symbolical as stories about the gods and their interactions with humans and the universe and nature, stories which at first sight resemble children's fairy tales, but when looked at closely reveal certain universal truths which later on a psychologist like Jung dubbed "archetypes of the human condition"; the journey archetype, for instance, being one of those.

This origin from the religious and the symbolical is often overlooked in modern theories on mythology. Dante's journey in the Divine Comedy is one concrete example of a mythological journey which remains tied to its religious origins, so is Homer's in the Odyssey, so is Captain Picard's journey on the Enterprise space ship; the journey is always a journey into the self looking for its origins and its final destination. They are certainly not historically documented journeys; they are more in the realm of the subjective, the imaginative and even that of the prophetic, more in the way of a myth, but a myth that repeats itself in many forms and among many people, even those who have no cultural contacts with each other, revealing a hidden deeper truth, a truth that goes beyond a mere empirical positivistic explanation of the visible material phenomena. We call them archetypes of the human condition. They may not be historically or empirically verifiable but they are certainly real since they exist in the realm of the intelligible just as logic, or mathematics, or astronomy are imbedded in the concrete materialistic positivistic realm of what is empirically verifiable; akin to religious faith of which one remains sure even when unable to prove it empirically.

Figure 4.5. The Journey of Ulysses in the Odyssey.

Figure 4.6. A Journey through the Universe.

Figure 4.7. An example of a mythological journey.

Campbell: Well put Plato. I couldn't agree with you more. I see that you have caught up and even surpassed us moderns in the understanding of the essence or nature of myth: it is not to be considered a lie, or the sugaring of the bitter pill of truth, as you put it when critiquing the bad poets, but a deeper truth to be decoded and reflected upon. That's basically what I try to do in my various books on mythology, especially the one titled "The Hero with a thousand Faces."

Plato: I have read all your books and they are illuminating on the subject of mythology. They invariably expand one's intellectual-spiritual horizon on the relationship of myth religion and reason.

Campbell: thank you for your kind words Plato, but could you indulge me a while more by explaining to me your summation of ancient Greek mythology mentioned by you, of Zeus splitting the human being in half so that from then on one half has been searching for the other half? Most scholars, including Jung, interpret that statement of yours via a biological metaphor as the masculine in search of the feminine looking for wholeness, but I suspect that there is much more to it.

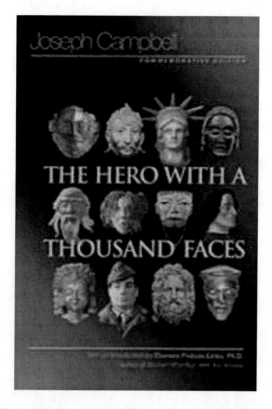

Figure 4.8. The faces of the hero as an archetype.

Plato: your suspicion is well founded, Joe. The Janus face represents the split which occurred when rationality overpowered the poetical and the mythological so that the poetical began to be defined as the deceptive which lies and puts sugar on the bitter truth of rationality to make it more bearable. Your modern philosopher Pascal points to this error with his statement that "the heart has reasons that reason knows not." Also there is another rather obscure but highly insightful philosopher of history, Giambattista Vico, from the 18th century, who identified the mistake of much of Western philosophy beginning with me, not only in its totalizing tendencies but in the attempt to subside the imaginative and the poetical under the rational and the empirical. The two belong together and have been searching for each other since they were split asunder by Positivism. He expresses all this in his masterpiece *The New Science (1725)*. When myth is split from the rational it becomes harmful, it ends up in myths such as that of "the master race." When reason is split from myth and the poetical it begins to rationalize and justify what ought never be rationalized. Indeed Pascal's and Vico's corrections, the corrections of two Christian humanists were very much needed for the ethical Western tradition as Emmanuel Levinas has also pointed out in the 20th century.

Figure 4.9. The Myth of Atlantis as described by Plato.

In the *Protagoras* I make a distinction between *muthos* and *logos*, where *muthos* appears to refer to a story and *logos* to an argument. This distinction is also echoed in the *Theaetetus* and the *Sophist*. In the *Theaetetus* Socrates discusses Protagoras' main doctrine and refers to it as "the *muthos* of Protagoras" Socrates there calls a *muthos* the teaching according to which active and passive motions generate perception and perceived objects. In the *Sophist*, the Visitor from Elea tells his interlocutors that Xenophanes, Parmenides and other Eleatic, Ionian (Heraclitus included) and Sicilian philosophers "appear to me to tell us a myth, as if we were children." By calling all those philosophical doctrines *muthoi* I do not claim that they are myths proper, but that they are, or appear to be, non-argumentative. In the *Republic* I may come across as fairly hostile to particular traditional myths. And in many dialogues I condemn the use of images in knowing things and claim that true philosophical knowledge should avoid images. But I ask you: does Book X of the *Republic* offer a single repudiation of the best poets of the Hellenic world? Try as you may, you will not find one. What you will find is a complicated counterpoint in which resistance and attraction to their work are intertwined, a counterpoint which (among other things) explores the problem of whether, and in what sense, it might be possible to be a 'philosophical lover' of poetry"

I wanted to persuade a wider audience, so I had to make a compromise. Sometime I use myth as a supplement to philosophical discourse Most importantly, in the *Timaeus,* I actually attempt to overcome the opposition between *muthos* and *logos*: human reason has limits, and when it reaches them it has to rely on myth. That is to say, the telling of stories is a necessary adjunct to, or extension of, philosophical argument, one which recognizes our human limitations, and—perhaps—the fact that our natures combine irrational elements with the rational"

Consider the fact that I chose to express my thoughts through a narrative form, namely that of the dialogue. So you may say that the use of a fictional narrative form (the dialogue, such as the one we are having right now) will mean that any conclusions reached, by whatever method (including that of 'rational argument'), may themselves be treated as having the status of a kind of myth. So, a sense of the fictionality of human utterance, as provisional, inadequate, and at best approximating to the truth, pervade my writing at its deepest level. It is not that myth fills in the gaps that reason leaves, but that human reason itself ineradicably displays some of the features we characteristically associate with story-telling.

Campbell: Wow! This is interesting stuff! It partly explains, to me at least, what a Catholic theologian expressed to me in a dispute we had once on "religion as myth." He told me that it may be true that religions are based on certain archetypes of human nature and myths of the human condition but to say that Christianity is just another myth to be disposed as all the other myths as lies and falsehoods to put a point across as we do with children's fairy tales, to be superseded by the scientific mind-set, is to have misunderstood the very nature of mythology which is there to help us better understand transcendental-revealed truths. That is to say, to use mythology as an excuse to dump religion as retrograde, obscurantist, and unenlightened, is to run the risk of throwing the baby with the bathwater out the window.

He also pointed out that Zeus or Atlas are impersonal ideas personified which when worshipped renders us idolaters or narcissists, but the concept of a benevolent providential creator God who takes on human nature to experience the human condition and enters physical reality historically and materially to redeem it is not a philosophical abstract idea to be found in any mythology; not even very intelligent philosophers like yourself ever thought of it; it is however the stuff of reality and historical events for which 12 ignorant fishermen from Palestine (no experts in Platonic or Socratic philosophy for which they'd be willing to die) were in fact willing to die because their allegiance was not to an idea but to a person who spiritually won the whole continent of Europe in a couple of centuries and gave it its ultimate identity as Judeo-Greco-Roman civilization; a religion this which makes a synthesis between the human and the divine and not only at an abstract theoretical level but at an existential level, and therefore it is humanistic to the core; that at its best advocates tolerance of other traditions, mythology itself, freedom of speech and democratic governance, given that we are all children of the same benevolent father and are commanded to love each other as brothers and sisters. I must admit that I am still chewing on what that theologian gave me to think about that day. I felt as if he had been check-mated in a chess game, but I don't think he was playing chess with me, out to win some kind of debate or diatribe. To the contrary, he simply challenged some of the common assumptions of "enlightened" positivistic modernity which were also mine.

Plato: well you should Joe, well you should. I am already ruminating on this whole conversation myself. While I do so, why don't we order another cognac and light up a pipe and start a game of chess? Perhaps take in a soccer game in the afternoon, since it happens to be Sunday?

Campbell: Indeed Plato, soccer games are now the new religion of the brave new world in which we live and have our being. Some call it the world of globalization. Some, perhaps more wisely, call it "reinventing the wheel," which come to think of it, can itself be a myth (the myth of Sisyphus?) and an archetype of the human condition. Have you ever noticed that the world of dreams has no Kantian rational categories of the understanding; it is not linear, nor strictly logical and rational and it needs plenty of interpretation once it is recollected? Could the Hindus, who are not even Westerners, have it on track when they say that we are all dreaming and when we die we will wake up to Reality, to the point of it all (the Word)?

Plato: I understand the concept of logos, but there are other things such as revealed truth and the need for forgiveness and the theological virtue of charity which I find difficult to grasp as an ancient philosopher; plenty of food for thought here; but it's only the antipasto announcing the main course. Let the debate go on.

Essay 5

THE IMMIGRANT "OTHER" IN US AND EU POLITICO-RELIGIOUS EXPERIENCES: A COMPARATIVE PERSPECTIVE

Figure 5.1. Refugees trying to get into Europe.

Can the EU welcome and integrate the immigrant "other"? Nowadays this urgent question is often asked by historians, sociologists, and political scientists. It has given rise to a plethora of books and academic conferences on the subject (see below for a sample). In the light of the events of the recent "refugee European crisis" the conclusions and prognosis are, more often than not, rather inconclusive and ineffective. In the short analysis that follows I'd like to examine the reasons for the deficiency, namely that the philosophy of religion is often ignored, if not downright excluded from the diagnosis, thus ending up with the wrong prognosis.

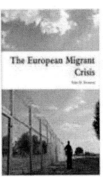

Appeared in 2016   Appeared in 2015

Figure 5.2. Recent books on the EU Migration Crisis.

Another aspect of the wrong diagnosis is the lack of comparative perspective on the issue. By that I mean a hard look at the immigrant experiences of both the American and European continents, preferably by scholars who have lived and worked on both sides of the Atlantic. After all, it was European societies that were the primary immigrant-sending regions to America, South Africa, Oceania and Australia and just about every corner of the globe during the colonial industrialization phase of their history (1700-1920); we are talking about some 85 million Europeans; some 60% of which emigrated to the Americas (some 50 millions).

Figure 5.3. Refugees fleeing to Europe.

The present paradox is that the flow has now reversed and several Western European societies have now in turn become centers of global immigration. A comparison is logical and in order. There may be hard lessons to be learned from it. There is now a ratio of approximately 10% immigrants living in several European countries (UK, France, Holland, West Germany, Italy). However, they still have difficulty viewing themselves as permanent immigrant societies, the way the US viewed and continues to view itself; or for that matter of viewing the native second generations as nationals irrespective of the legal status of their citizenship. A de facto, second rate citizenship seems to be in place. The question arises: Why is that?

This question can only be answered by analyzing how these Western European countries have tried to accommodate immigrant religions, particularly Islam. Although European laws and regulations are now in place, each nation, deals with immigrant religions in markedly different institutional and legal structures on how the immigrants may publicly express religious beliefs and practices. Here a thorough knowledge of modern Western European history vis a vis religion can be useful in assessing the different reactions of various EU nations.

The French model of *laicitè* (or secularism) is primary in this respect. In practice secularism means a strict privatization of religion, its elimination from the public forum, while pressuring religious groups to organize themselves into a single centralized churchlike structure and serve as intermediary between it and the state, so as to better regulate and manipulate it. The model is in part the concordat with the Catholic Church established in Italy in 1929. Religion is tolerated but it is a private matter even when its symbols are pervasive in the country's traditional culture. A great wall of separation between Church and State exists, as indeed is also the case in the US whose founding fathers well remembered the disastrous European wars of religions of the 17th century.

Figure 5.4. The Concordat of 1929 between Italy and the Church.

Great Britain, by contrast, while maintaining the established Church of England, allows greater freedom to religious associations, who deal directly with local authorities and school boards to press for changes in religious education, diet, etc., with little direct appeal to the central government. Germany, following the multi-establishment model, has tried to organize a quasi-official Islamic institution, at times in conjunction with parallel strivings on the part of the Turkish state to regulate its diaspora.

But the internal divisions among immigrants from Turkey, as well as the public expression and mobilization of competing identities (secular and Muslim, Alevi and Kurd) in the German democratic context, have undermined any project of institutionalization from above. Holland, following its traditional pattern of pillarization, seemed, at least until very recently, bent on establishing a separate state-regulated but self-organized Muslim pillar. Lately, however, even traditionally liberal and tolerant Holland is expressing second thoughts, and seems ready to pass more restrictive legislation setting clear limits to the kinds of un-European, un-modern norms and habits it is prepared to tolerate.

But let us now look more closely at the comparison between the EU and the US. If one looks at the European Union as a whole, there are two fundamental differences with the situation in the United States. In Europe, first of all, immigration and Islam are almost synonymous. The overwhelming majority of immigrants in most European countries, the UK being the main exception, are Muslims, and the overwhelming majority of Western European Muslims are immigrants. This identification appears even more pronounced in those cases where the majority of Muslim immigrants tend to come predominantly from a single region, e.g., Turkey in the case of Germany, the Ma'ghreb in the case of France. This entails a superimposition of different dimensions of "otherness" that exacerbates issues of boundaries, accommodation and incorporation. The immigrant, the religious, the racial, and the socio-economic de-privileged "other" all tend to coincide.

In the United States, on the other hand, Muslims constitute at most 10 percent of all new immigrants. it is estimated that from 30 to 42 percent of all Muslims in the United States are African-American converts to Islam, making the characterization of Islam as a foreign, un-American religion even more difficult. The dynamics of interaction with other Muslim immigrants, with African-American Muslims, with non-Muslim immigrants from the same regions of origin, and with their immediate American hosts are, depending on socio-economic characteristics and residential patterns, much more complex and diverse than anything one finds in Europe. A nuance this which escapes the simple-minded approach of a Donald Trump and his cohorts.

Figure 5.5. Muslim American.

The second main difference has to do with the role of religion and religious group identities in public life and in the organization of civil society. Western European societies are deeply secular societies, shaped by the hegemonic knowledge regime of secularism. As liberal democratic societies, they tolerate and respect individual religious freedom. But due to the increasing pressure towards the privatization of religion, which among European societies is now taken for granted as a characteristic of the self-definition of modern secular society, those societies have much greater difficulty in offering a legitimate role for religion in public life, and in the organization and mobilization of collective group identities. Muslim organized collective identities and their public representations become a source of anxiety, not only because of their religious otherness as a non-Christian and non-European religion, but, even more significantly, because of their religiousness itself as the "other" of European secularity. Presently, a post-secular Europe as envisioned by the German philosopher Jurgen Habermas, is not on the horizon yet, if anything, things are going from bad to worse with the advent of right-wing ultra-nationalistic parties resurgent all over Europe and threatening the democratic system buttressed by Christian principles as envisioned by the EU founding fathers, the likes of Aedenauer, Schuman, Monet, De Gasperi, etc.

Figure 5.6. Signing of the EU Constitution in Rome on the 29th of October 2004.

In this context, the temptation to identify Islam and fundamentalism becomes all the more pronounced. Islam, by definition, becomes the other of Western secular modernity allegedly rooted in a universal European enlightenment. Therefore, the problems posed by the incorporation of Muslim immigrants become consciously or unconsciously associated with seemingly related and vexatious issues concerning the role of religion in the public sphere, which is a question European societies assumed they had already solved according to the liberal secular norm of the privatization of religion. The assumption has resulted premature.

Americans, by contrast, are demonstrably more religious than Europeans. Therefore there is a certain pressure for immigrants to conform to American religious norms. It is generally the case that immigrants in America tend to be more religious than they were in their home countries. I can attest to this on a personal level: I do not remember my parents attending Church on a regular basis on Sunday in Italy while they did so once they emigrated to America. I am quite sure such was the case for my grandparents once they emigrated to New York where my father was born in 1912.

Figure 5.7. An immigrant arriving in America at the beginning of the 20th century.

But even more significantly, today as in the past, religion and public religious denominational identities play an important role in the process of incorporating new immigrants. The thesis of Will Herberg concerning the old European immigrant, that "not only was he expected to retain his old religion, as he was not expected to retain his old language or nationality, but such was the shape of America that it was largely in and through religion that he, or rather his children and grandchildren, found an identifiable place in American life," is still operative with the new immigrants. The thesis implies that collective religious identities have been one of the primary ways of structuring internal societal pluralism in American history.

Due to the corrosive logic of racialization, so pervasive in American society, the dynamics of religious identity formation assume a double positive form in the process of immigrant incorporation. Given the institutionalized acceptance of religious pluralism, the affirmation of religious identities is enhanced among the new immigrants. This positive affirmation is reinforced, moreover, by what appears to be a common defensive reaction by most immigrant groups against ascribed racialization, particularly against the stigma of racial darkness. In this respect, religious and racial self-identifications and ascriptions represent alternative ways of organizing American multiculturalism. One of the obvious advantages of religious pluralism over racial pluralism is that, under proper constitutional institutionalization, it is more reconcilable with principled equality and non-hierarchic diversity, and therefore with genuine multiculturalism.

American society is indeed entering a new phase. The traditional model of assimilation, turning European nationals into American "ethnics," can no longer serve as a model of assimilation now that immigration is literally worldwide. America is bound to become "the first new global society" made up of all world religions and civilizations, at a time when religious civilizational identities are regaining prominence at the global level. At the very same moment that political scientists like Samuel Huntington are announcing the impending clash of civilizations in global politics, a new experiment in intercivilizational encounters and accommodation between all the world religions is taking place at home. American religious pluralism is expanding and incorporating all the world religions in the same way as it previously incorporated the religions of the old immigrants. A complex process of mutual accommodation is taking place. Like Catholicism and Judaism before, other world religions, Islam, Hinduism, Buddhism are being "Americanized" and in the process they are transforming American religion, while, much as American Catholicism had an impact upon the transformation of world Catholicism and American Judaism has transformed world Judaism, the religious diasporas in America are serving as catalysts for the transformation of the old religions in their civilizational homes.

This process of institutionalization of expanding religious pluralism is facilitated by the dual clause of the First Amendment which guarantees "no establishment" of religion at the state level, and therefore the strict separation of church and state and the genuine neutrality of the secular state, as well as the "free exercise" of religion in civil society. The latter includes strict restrictions on state intervention and on the administrative regulation of the religious field. It is this combination of a rigidly secular state and the constitutionally protected free exercise of religion in society that distinguishes the American institutional context from the European one. In Europe one finds, on the one extreme, the case of France, where a secularist state not only restricts and regulates the exercise of religion in society but actually imposes its republican ideology of *laïcité* on society, and, on the other, the case of England, where an established state church is compatible with wide toleration of religious minorities and the relatively unregulated free exercise of religion.

As liberal democratic systems, all European societies respect the private exercise of religion, including Islam, as an individual human right. It is the public and collective free exercise of Islam as an immigrant religion that most European societies find difficult to tolerate, precisely on the grounds that Islam is perceived as an "un-European" religion. The stated rationales for considering Islam "un-European" vary significantly across Europe, and among social and political groups. For the anti-immigrant, xenophobic, nationalist Right, represented by Le Pen's discourse in France and Jörg Haider's in Austria, the message is straightforward: Islam is unwelcome and un-assimilable, simply because it is a "foreign" immigrant religion. Such a nativist and usually racist attitude can be differentiated clearly from the conservative "Catholic" position, paradigmatically expressed by the Cardinal of Bologna when he declared that Italy should welcome immigrants of all races and regions of the world, but should particularly select Catholic immigrants in order to preserve the country's Catholic identity.

Sad to say, when it comes to Islam, secular Europeans usually liberal in their views on religion in general, tend to reveal the limits and prejudices of modern secularist toleration. The politically correct formulation tends to run along such lines as "we welcome each and all immigrants irrespective of race or religion as long as they are willing to respect and accept our modern liberal secular European norms." Revealingly enough, some time ago Prime Minister Jean-Pierre Raffarin, in his address to the French legislature defending the banning of ostensibly religious symbols in public schools, made reference in the same breath to France as "the old land of Christianity" and to the inviolable principle of *laïcité*, exhorting Islam to adapt itself to the principle of secularism as all other religions of France have done before. "For the most recently arrived, I'm speaking here of Islam, secularism is a chance, the chance to be a religion of France." The Islamic veil and other religious signs are justifiably banned from public schools, he added, because "they are taking on a political meaning," while according to the secularist principle of privatization of religion, "religion cannot be a political project." Time will tell whether the restrictive legislation will have the intended effect of stopping the spread of "radical Islam," or whether it is likely to bring forth the opposite result of further radicalizing an already alienated and maladjusted immigrant community.

The positive rationale one hears among liberals in support of such illiberal restrictions on the free exercise of religion is usually put in terms of the desirable enforced emancipation of young girls, against their expressed will if necessary, from gender discrimination and patriarchal control. This was the discourse on which the assassinated liberal politician Pim Fortuyn built his electorally successful anti-immigrant platform in liberal Holland, a campaign that is now bearing fruit in new restrictive legislation. While conservative religious persons are expected to tolerate behavior they may consider morally abhorrent such as homosexuality, liberal secular Europeans are openly stating that European societies ought not to tolerate religious behavior or cultural customs that are morally abhorrent, insofar as they are contrary to modern liberal secular European norms. What makes the intolerant tyranny of the secular liberal majority justifiable in principle is not just the democratic principle of majority rule, but the secularist teleological assumption, built into theories of modernization, that one set of norms is reactionary, fundamentalist and anti-modern, while the other is progressive, liberal and modern.

In conclusion, from the above considerations and reflections, we can safely assume that sociological-historical considerations, while helpful for the analysis of the issue of religion vis a vis the secular "enlightened" state, are not sufficient by themselves to arrive at a proper diagnosis and prognosis of the problem. What is also needed, and is solely missing in the ongoing dialogue, is an analysis that takes seriously and incorporates the philosophy of religion. Without a philosophy of religion the analysis and consequently the prognosis will continue to remain incomplete and ineffective. But let the dialogue continue among people of good will, be they believers or non-believers.

Essay 6

EIGHT SCHOLARS' VIEWS (DANTE, HUSSERL, LEVINAS, DAWSON, WEILER, HABERMAS, EISENSTADT AND TROELTSCH) ON THE LOSS OF EUROPEAN SPIRITUAL IDENTITY

Clearly the title Europe designates the unity of a spiritual life and creative activity--no matter how inimical the European nations may be toward each other, still they have a special inner affinity of spirit that permeates all of them and transcends their national differences... There is an innate entelechy that thoroughly controls the changes in the European image and directs it toward an ideal image of life and of being. The spirited telos of the European in which is included the particular telos of separate nations and individual persons, has an infinity; it is an infinite idea toward which in secret the collective spiritual becoming, so to speak, strives.

--Edmund Husserl

Figure 6.1. Eight scholars of the EU cultural identity.

I

The renowned Church historian Ernst Troeltsch once boldly declared that Europe had ceased to be Christian in the 18th century. Of course such a statement referred not to individuals but to the cultural identity of Europe as a whole. Some post-modern thinkers not only would wholly agree with that statement but would also point out that indeed the 18th century is the watershed separating Christendom, so called, or the old Europe, and the new modern Europe. This New Europe, after World War II has finally transformed itself in the European Union and is based on purely neutral, that is to say, non-ideological, economic, scientific, educational foundations.

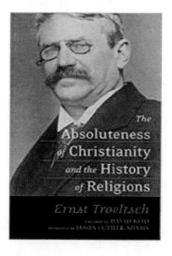

Figure 6.2. A great scholar of religions.

This leads to a crucial question: are those foundations reliable and solid enough by themselves, or is there something sorely missing? Is the absence of spiritual foundations a sign that a more perfect union transcending nationalism will forever elude the European Union? Some post-modern philosophers attribute the problem of modernity to a mistake made at the beginning of Western culture, to Plato in particular. They assume a continuity between modern rationalism and the principles of reason as formulated by the ancient Greeks. Others draw a distinction between the original principles of rationality and their modern interpretation. They trace the root of that distinction, with its dramatic political implications, to the modern turn toward the human subject as the only source of truth and its consequent pragmatism. This turn was initiated, to be precise, by Renè Descartes, widely considered the father of modern Western philosophy.

What post-modern thinkers reject is not only Enlightenment rationalism, but also the original Greek form of rationality. For them rationality is little more than behavioral attitudes, a sort of incessant self-correction and perfectibility patterned after the experimentalism and self-correction of science. This is considered progress. In fact, it is branded as deterministic inevitable progress: the newest is always the best. Allegedly, it does away with disastrous and destructive universalist totalizing ideologies, the grand scheme of things a la Hegel, the grand narrations, often at war with each other. The argument is this: it is better to be more modest in one's goals and humbly attend to immediate social and economic needs. Welcome Epicurus and Lucretius, away with Plato's grandiose Forms. What is conveniently side-stepped are some fundamental issues at which we shall look a bit more closely.

Indeed, the ineluctable fact is that Europeans no longer agree on spiritual values; those values that, despite political conflicts, were in place prior to the Enlightenment. It took the Czech philosopher Jan Patocka (who in turn greatly influenced Havel) to dare propose, in the middle of the 20th century, a return to an idea that used to be characteristic of the European tradition since the Greeks but in the 20th century is seen as a scandal and an anomaly: the care of the soul by way of a great respect for truth and the intellectual life, holistically conceived. Plato had claimed that it is through such a life that we, as human beings endowed with a soul, partake of the life of the Ideas and share the life of the gods themselves. Later, Christians adopt this notion but change its direction. For Christians, theoria, or contemplation, remains the fundamental principle of any viable culture. Bereft of it, a civilization is left with nothing but a sort of aimless and blind praxis leading to its eventual destruction. Christopher Dawson for one explored and clarified this idea in his famous *The Making of Europe*.

Eight Scholars' Views ... 53

Figure 6.3. Patocka who revived the idea of the care of the soul.

So, the next question is this: can such a principle as advocated by Plato play a role in the spiritual unification of Europe? Which is to say, must the commitment to reason abandon a sort of rationalistic universalism that opposes it to an anti-rationalist particularism? To deepen a bit more: is not abstract rationalism and its irrational reaction to it responsible for much of the ominous nihilism which Nietzsche, for one, claimed hovers over Europe like a menacing specter? Has it not, in fact, corrupted the very principle of reason that, up to the Enlightenment, had constituted Europe's spiritual identity? Has it not turned wisdom against itself? Prior to World War II, the philosopher who most acutely perceived the spiritual crisis that rationalism has caused in Europe was Edmund Husserl. In a famous lecture delivered in Prague on the very eve of one of the darkest chapters of modern European history, he said this: "I too am quite sure that the European crisis has its roots in a mistaken rationalism. That, however, must not be interpreted as meaning that rationality as such is an evil or that in the totality of human existence it is of minor importance.

The rationality of which alone we are speaking is rationality in that noble genuine sense, the Greek sense, that became an ideal in the classical period of Greek philosophy. All we need to do is give a cursory look at Husserl's philosophy of phenomenology to be convinced that Husserl regarded modern objectivism as the quintessential expression of this rationalism. It reduces the world, which for the Greeks was a spiritual structure, into an object, and reason into an instrument for manipulating matter. One may ask, how then did Husserl view the spiritual identity of Europe? As the quote by him on top of this essay implies, he advocated that the particular must be fully reintegrated with the universal, the immanent with the transcendent, an idea this that Kierkegaard too had proposed and before him Vico and after him Maurice Blondel; all renowned scholars in the philosophy of religion.

Vico   Kierkegaard   Blondel
(1668-1744)   (1813-1855)   (1861-1949)

Figure 6.4. Three philosophers of religion and history.

But the question persists: is it possible at this point in its history to revive the spiritual idea of Europe? An idea that, despite Europe incessant wars, has kept its people united within an unrestricted diversity? Food for thought, to be duly digested by those of us who, like Husserl, are perceptive enough to sense the spiritual crisis he was talking about. In his

Philosophical Discourse on Modernity Jurgen Habermas attributes the failure of the Enlightenment to the intrusion of foreign elements which derailed its original program of full human emancipation. He finds nothing wrong with the project itself, aside from the fact that it was prematurely abandoned for a romantic return to some form of pseudo-religion, such as the worship of nature in the 19th century, the era of Romanticism. Undoubtedly there is something unfinished about the Enlightenment, but contrary to what Habermas believes, it is not the execution of the project that failed to reach a conclusion but the concept itself had a flaw. Many question nowadays the very principle of rationality that directed Enlightenment thought. This may sound paradoxical, for indeed it is the adoption of reason by the Greeks and the subsequent synthesis with Christianity as achieved by Augustine and Aquinas that distinguishes European culture from all others and defines its spiritual identity.

St. Thomas Aquinas (1225-1274)

St. Augustine of Hippo (354-430 AD)

Figure 6.5. Augustinie and Aquinas helped in the synthesis of Faith and Reason.

To be sure, the real culprit was not reason or rationality but rationalism, which was unknown to the Greeks. Rationalism is a modern invention inaugurated by Descartes and consisting in a separation of the particular from the universal and assigning supremacy to the universal while misguidedly assuming that a rationality constituted by the human mind could function as the same comprehensive principle that it had been for the Greeks. To the contrary, a rationality of purely subjective origin produces mere abstract, empty concepts in theory and pursues limited human objectives in practice, mostly narrowly focused upon economic, scientific, and political concerns. Einstein had it on target: our era is characterized by perfection of means and confusion of goals.

Figure 6.6. Renè Descartes (1596-1650).

Indeed, in developed societies where economic concerns have become all-important and dominant, the protection of sub-national identities and minority groups are at risk. One place where any obstacle to economic development has been successfully eliminated is the United States, usually mentioned as a model of federalism encompassing many nationalities. Many EU politicians advocate a United States of Europe. That may sound progressive, but it remains a chimera given that the nationalistic and regional identities are still very strong in Europe; nor is it necessarily desirable. One thinks of Catalonia, Corsica, the Tyrol region of Italy. It would be a mistake for the EU to imitate the US and attempt a repetition of a mega-nation which would translate into a super-power bent on power and the forcible exportation of democracy (an oxymoron if there ever was one).

The price that will have to be paid will be further erosion of Europe's original spiritual unifying principles, the very roots of its cultural identity, and the embracing of a bland mixture of varied cultures leveled to its least common denominator. Soccer games heralded as a unifying principle may indeed be emblematic of that mistake. What some Europeans fail to grasp is that what keeps so many ethnic nationalities and groups together in the US is a constitution based on ethical ideals and principles which guarantees certain basic rights transcending nationality and even the very power of the State in as much as they are conceived as inalienable, not based on raw power, but on the very nature of man. Those enshrined ideals are what makes "a pluribus unum" possible, as the dollar bill proclaims.

It will prove difficult for Europeans with different languages reflecting diverse cultures to create a United States of Europe, nor should they. As it is, all the worst features of American popular culture are being imitated, even by those who are anti-Americans, while the best is largely unknown or ignored. That is not to deny that one of the major achievements of the European Union has been the preventing of a major destructive conflict on the continent at the level of a world war for the last sixty years or so. By itself such an achievement makes the forming of some kind of union well worth it. However, to count on mere political-economic motives to completely free Europe from its past destructive legacies may well be a miscalculation.

Calling oneself a "Newropean" born in original innocence in 1951 and oblivious of his history will not do the trick either. It would suffice to take a hard look at the xenophobia that has raised its ugly head and pervades the EU especially its most affluent countries and the countries that were the original founders. Superficially it seems directed at immigrants coming from outside Europe, especially Muslims, but often the real target is a neighboring country. What seems to be lacking within this economic, political, educational coordination that is the EU is a deeper kind of integration based on an inclusive spiritual idea. How is this to be achieved in a secular democratic society pledged to protect the rights of all its citizens and their diversity? A nostalgic return to the Greek-Christian synthesis and the Christendom of medieval times, so called Christendom a la Charlemagne (at times imposed politically) will not do either, and is not even desirable. That was a synthesis meant for Europeans Christians (many of them forced to get baptized by their kings who found it politically convenient to switch from paganism to Christianity), not for non-Christians, not to speak of the non-Europeans which are now counted into the millions in many countries of Europe. In any case, it is undeniable that at present no strong spiritual foundation for a genuine unification exists.

The present fought over Constitution which nobody even calls constitution any longer but a compact, mentions a fuzzy kind of spiritual heritage almost as an after-thought. Many Europeans don't seem to be too concerned about such an absence, if indeed they even perceive it. The prophetic words of the former pope John Paul II to the European parliament in 1979 that to ignore such a legacy is to ensure a non-viable future to European man, were all but ignored. And yet, some kind of new synthesis is needed. Unfortunately, it will not even be envisioned, never mind implemented, unless Europeans, begin a serious reflection and a debate on the original idea to which Europe owes its cultural unity and identity. That carries the risk of being perceived as an old-fashion European, maybe even an anti-modern and anti-progressive one, rather than a "Newropean," but I would suggest that without that original idea, which precedes Christianity itself, a crucial novantiqua synthesis will not be perceived either, and Europeans will be sadly condemned to repeat their history.

What is this European original foundational spiritual idea that precedes even Christianity? Simply this: a commitment to theoria, the theoretical life which in its Greek etymology means the contemplative or reflective life in all its various aspects: the philosophical, the scientific, the aesthetic; in short the primacy of a holistic life of contemplation. All this sounds strange to modern and post-modern ears accustomed to hear praxis and a purely pragmatic technological notion of rationality emphasized over and above theory. Marx, for one, expressed such a mind-set in the 11th of the Theses on Feuerbach with this catch-all slogan: "The philosophers have only interpreted the world differently, the point is to change it." Indeed, but to start with praxis is to put the cart before the horse.

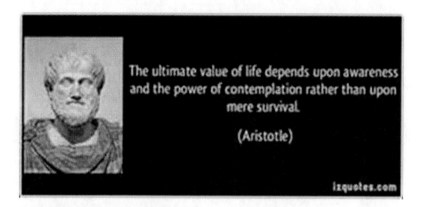

Figure 6.7. Man is a rational animal.

Unfortunately, postmodern theories, in an attempt to reject an extreme kind of rationalism, have also rejected the primacy of reason understood holistically and tied to the imaginative, which had ruled Western thought since the Greeks. Precisely the belief in that primacy, together with a common faith that could envision the transcendent and join it to the immanent, had been one of the spiritual foundations of Europe. It was that kind of devaluation and departure from foundational traditions that Husserl was decrying before World War II. Here the question naturally arises: is it still possible to revive the ideals behind Europe's spiritual identity?

If this requires returning to a common Christian faith and to a pre-modern concept of reason, it will prove practically impossible. Science demands a more differentiated notion of reason than the one inherent in ancient and medieval thought. As for the common Christian faith that forged such a strong bond among Europe's peoples, many Europeans have lost it, if they ever had it, and most recent immigrants, many of them Muslims never had it to begin with. This is not to forget that Moslem civilization in Spain during the Middle Ages was more developed and advanced than a Western civilization devastated by the Barbarians. Does the above reflection intimate perhaps that Europe must be satisfied with a merely political, technical, scientific, and economic integration? Such a spiritually "neutral" union does indeed appear to be "enlightened" in as much as it avoids the unfortunate conflicts of the past. Furthermore, many Europeans today think that social and cultural differences obstruct or slow down the process of economic growth and social progress. Why, then, don't all Europeans adopt English as the common language for science, business, and technology, leaving French, Italian, Spanish, German, Dutch, and Scandinavian languages to private life?

Figure 6.8. Medieval Islamic Spain.

Again, this may sound strange to post-modern ears, but if the European Union were reduced to a means for smoothing out political and economic transactions among its member states, not only would the individual states, not to speak of regions, gradually lose their cultural identity, they would also be doomed to play a very subordinate role on the world stage in the future. Even today, only a half century after the United States has economically and politically come to dominate the world, its powerful media and commercial enterprises have deeply affected the languages, the communications, and the cultural patterns of Europe. The effect is most visible in the smaller nations. Thus in the Low Countries the language of the news media has become infected with American idioms, bookstores are filled with American publications or translations thereof, television and cinema compete for the most recent American shows or films—all this at the expense of linguistic purity and respect for indigenous literature. Even the bigger countries like Italy and Spain can hardly contain the tidal wave of American popular culture. The result is a general decline of native creativity. What is even more perplexing is that what is being imitated is not the best of American culture (which is there if one takes the trouble to diligently look for it) but the worst and the mediocre.

Be that as it may, whoever controls the economy of another country is likely to control its culture as well, as Benjamin, Adorno and Marx have well taught us. Building a strong economy of one's own, as Europe has been doing, is a necessary step to resisting such domination. But that alone may not be sufficient. If the European Union were to be reduced to a mere economic union, its leveling effect on European culture would in the end be comparable to the one the United States has begun to exercise. We are all Americans because we all drink Coke; and we are all Europeans because we all go to soccer games on Sunday! To the contrary, Europe's political and economic unification must be accompanied by a strong awareness of a distinctive cultural and spiritual identity. This is the reason why the dispute over Europe's Christian heritage is so important. In writing the preamble to the EU constitution, the most significant element in the European tradition is erased at the peril of building on political sand, as Kurt Held reminded us in his essay on Europe titled "The Origins of Europe with the Greek Discovery of the World," with the following words: "A European community grounded only in political and economic cooperation of the member states would lack an intrinsic common bond. It would be built upon sand."

The American techno-economic model of a political union is not suitable for Europe, especially of a Europe which has forgotten its spiritual roots and in the past has substituted them with political ideologies. Being a new country, with immigrants from various traditions, the United States had no choice but to build politically on a spiritually and culturally neutral foundation but the strict separation of Church and State in the US is deceiving. Its spiritual roots remained strong and were in fact a unifying principle. This base enabled the United States to integrate the economy and the social institutions of its states into a strong and coherent unity that resulted in the most powerful nation in history. This is not to deny that the glue that held the uniform structure together were indeed the ideals of the Enlightenment (but ultimately based on a Judeo-Christian ethos) as enshrined in its Constitution.

Figure 6.9. Francesco Petrarca: Father of Humanism (1304-1374).

There is a lesson there for Europe to be pondered carefully before embracing a knee-jerk and mindless anti-Americanism or, even worse, a slavish imitation of all the worst features of American culture. Contemporary Europeans have preserved their diverse languages, customs, and histories, even at the regional level, and that points to an appreciation for tradition and heritage which is indispensable for a strong cultural identity. But, to reiterate, Europe needs a strong spiritual reintegration as well as a political-economic one. That requires that it assimilate essential parts of its spiritual heritage: the Greek sense of order and measure, the Roman respect for law, the biblical and Christian care for the other person, the humanitas of Renaissance humanism, the ideals of political equality and individual rights of the Enlightenment. The values left by each of these episodes of Western culture are not as transient as the cultures in which they matured. They belong permanently to Europe's spiritual patrimony and ought to remain constitutive of its unity. None can be imposed in a democratic society. Yet none may be neglected either, the theoretical no more than the practical, the spiritual no less than the aesthetic.

In recent times Europeans, discouraged by the self-made disasters of two world wars, have been too easily inclined to turn their backs on the past, to dismiss it as no longer usable, and to move toward a different future declaring themselves "Newropeans" with a new identity. In the years after World War II, the model of that future was America. In recent years, Europeans have become more conscious of their specific identity and are beginning to intuit that such an identity resides in the past; it stems from a unique past, created by the hundreds of millions of men and women who for three millennia have lived on "that little cape on the continent of Asia" (Paul Valery) between the North Sea and the Mediterranean, between Ireland's west coast and the Ural Mountains. It has given Europeans, in all their variety, a distinct communal face. This new awareness of cultural identity makes Europeans view the entire continent and its many islands, not only their country of origin, as a common homeland with common purposes. This unity of spirit in a rich variety of expressions must be remembered in forging the new European unity and ought to be mentioned in the EU's constitution. Its Constitution ought to have a preamble with a vision that inspires the people. That vision cannot be only economic and political but is necessarily a spiritual one. Without that kind of cement the whole edifice will eventually crumble. It goes without saying that it ought to be remembered also by North Americans whose roots are indeed Europeans; in that sense they too are also Westerners and inheritor of Western civilization, albeit accepting and integrating other experiences such as the African, the Native American, the Latin-American, the Asian. If all of this sounds too utopian and unpractical, I ask, what are the alternatives? I propose that a conspiracy of hope, as utopian as it may sound, is always preferable to the cynicism of a desperate nihilism. Europa, nosce te ipsum!

II

There is a rather naïve notion that the vision of a politically United Europe was born ex nihilo in 1950. The notion is naïve because it loses sight of the fact that there is no such thing in history as creations out of nothing. We stand on the shoulders of giants. It is therefore both proper and fitting to remember and celebrate those European cultural giants who, after the fall of the Roman Empire, began envisioning a United Europe.

Figure 6.10. Botticelli's Primavera: A Renaissance synthesis of Antiquity and Christianity.

As a Christian humanist Dante exemplifies the synthesis of Antiquity (i.e., Greco-Roman civilization) with Christianity. The mere fact that he chose Virgil, the poet of Latinity, as his guide in the Commedia, hints at it. With that synthesis Dante becomes the poet of the Italians just as Virgil had been the poet of the Romans. By giving them a written literature (The Divine Comedy) he gives them a national language and a cultural identity. There is a passage in The Divine Comedy where Dante is transported in spirit above the vicissitudes of men and flies higher and higher in the blue sky till he sees the earth just as 20th century astronauts saw it from the moon. I suppose that makes Dante the first global space walker, albeit via imagination.

Two intriguing characteristics in this passage are worthy of notice: in the first place Dante does not discern any geographical or political borders on the earth: he sees the whole earth, holistically, so to speak, just as the astronauts saw it from the moon in 1969. Thereafter Dante comments that "vidi quell'aiuola che ci fa tanto selvaggi" which translates loosely as "I saw that puny garden that makes us so vicious." He is addressing not just the Florentines or the Italians, or the Europeans but the whole of humankind. In effect Dante with this contrast of good/bad, ugly/beautiful, true/false, puny/precious, is saying that this unique earth which is Man's only home within time and space is meant to be beautiful as a garden, at the outset, but the sad ugly present reality is that in this garden brother kills brother; it is one of general viciousness and incessant warfare. Dante is pointing out that this garden is a garden of exile and humankind's journey is a journey back to the future, a journey of a return toward that utopist garden it originally left behind. Later in his imaginary journey Dante will enter the earthly garden of Eden on top of the mountain of Purgatory, but his journey transcends even that beautiful earthly garden.

It is crucial to remember here that Dante, as he writes the Commedia, is himself in exile. He has been expelled from his beloved Florence because there too brother is fighting brother; Ghibellines are fighting Guelfs. Dante used to be a Guelf; they were divided in the Blacks who saw in the Pope an ally against the Emperor (Henry VII of Germany at the time), and the Whites who were determined to remain fiercely independent of both Pope and Emperor. When the Blacks, supported by Pope Boniface VIII (later placed in hell by Dante for politicizing his spiritual mission) seize power, Dante, as a White, is sent into exile. It is this condition of exile, of constant frustration of having "to eat the hard bread of others' homes," of constant hardship and uneasiness and dissatisfaction, that propels Dante into a spiritual quest aptly depicted in the Commedia and ending with his famous "tua volontà, nostra pace" (your will, our peace).

Had he stayed in Florence he would have remained just another self-complacent mediocre politician. The experience of exile transforms Dante and his political views; he ends up embracing the cause of the Ghibellines and begins to champion the unification of Europe under an enlightened Emperor. He writes a Latin political tract titled "De Monarchia" where this vision is set forth. Dante has now come full circle, from the particularity of his city of Florence he is now envisioning a Europe unified by universal ideals such as justice, peace, the common good, the True, the Good, the Beautiful; ideals to be privileged above and beyond mere Machiavellian power considerations. His is a Humanistic political ethic founded on universal Christian principles.

Figure 6.11. Dante and his Divine Comedy.

The Europe that Dante envisions in De Monarchia is one that keeps a strict separation between Church and State (what Italians now call "lo stato laico") so that which is Caesar's will be given to Caesar and that which is God's will be given to God. That means religious freedom and tolerance for other faiths and traditions such as the Moslem, fully welcomed at the Court of Frederick II in Palermo which greatly influenced Italian culture. Italy will be just another country among European countries and its preeminence will consist less on its militaristic Roman heritage, and more on its Humanistic foundations.

Dante is therefore one of the grandfathers of this vision of a United Europe. As the consummate poet he is, he reminds all Europeans that, in the words of the Dante scholar, the British-American poet T.S. Eliot, "...The end of all our exploring will be to arrive where we started from and know the place for the first time." At that place we shall rediscover "l'amor che move il sole e l'altre stelle" [The love that moves the sun and the other stars]—Paradiso XXXIII, 145.

III

"I am quite sure that the European crisis has its roots in a mistaken rationalism"

--Edmund Husserl, University of Prague, 1935)

Modern Western Civilization presents us with a Janus-like face: On one side Renaissance Humanism which begins in Italy in the 14th century with Petrarch, on the other side Enlightenment Rationalism which begins in France in the 17th century with Descartes. After Descartes, there is a dangerous tendency to separate the two cultural phenomena and consider Humanism either anachronistic, or superseded. The inevitable result has been sheer confusion in the area of cultural identity; consequently, at this critical juncture of the new polity called European Union, there is talk of a "democratic deficit," that democracy that is integral part of Western Civilization. We are in urgent need of cultural guides to show us how to better harmonize the two above mentioned phenomena. One such guide is Emmanuel Lévinas' humanistic philosophy. In as much as it challenges the Western rationalistic philosophical tradition, it is extremely important for the emergence of a renewed European cultural identity. It explores in depth the threats to the authentic cultural identity of Europe, how modalities of thinking powerfully affect other ideas and shape a whole cultural milieu, sometimes with less than desirable consequences.

Figure 6.12. Levinas' Ph.D. dissertation.

A few background biographical details may be useful to better understand Lévinas. He was born in Lithuania in 1902. In 1923 he moves to Strasbourg to study under Husserl and writes a doctoral dissertation on his philosophy. There, he also comes in contact with Heidegger's philosophy. The dissertation on Husserl's phenomenology gets published in France in 1930 and reveals that, even at this early stage, Lévinas is beginning to take his distance from Heidegger. He enlisted in the French army, was captured in 1940 and spent the remaining five years of the war in two prisoner-of-war camps. Upon being liberated he returns to Lithuania and finds-out that his parents and siblings had been killed by the Nazis, while his wife, whom he had left behind in Paris, had survived thanks to the help of French nuns who hid her. He became a teacher and administrator in an institute for Jewish education in Paris (l'alliance Uneversel Juif); there he begins to study traditional Jewish texts under the directorship of the Talmudic sage Mordechai Shoshani to whom Elie Wiesel (who also studied with him) devotes a chapter in Legends of Our Time. In 1961 Lévinas defends the first of his two major philosophical works (Totality and Infinity) before the philosophy faculty of the Sorbonne becoming a professor of philosophy. His second major work bears the title of Otherwise than Being or Beyond Essence.

Those are the basic events that dramatically change Lèvinas' thinking. Prior to World War II he had merely criticized elements of 20th century Western thought; afterward he begins to attack the whole European philosophical tradition, especially its culmination in Heidegger's thought, for what he considers its indifference to the ethical and its "totalizing of the other." He begins to indict western philosophers in general for an uncritical reliance on vast concepts, such as Hegel's "Spirit," or Heidegger's "Being," which assimilate countless individuals to rational processes, thus negating their individuality. To be sure Kierkegaard had also criticized this Hegelian tendency, countering it with his existentialist philosophy. Those who understood his critique only too well, promptly proceeded to relegate his thought to the theological within a false dichotomy (shown absurd by Thomas Aquinas way back in the 13th century) of philosophy/theology, thus insuring that Kierkegaard would never be as influential as a Hegel or a Heidegger. In any case, Lévinas too argues that this taken-for-granted totalizing mode of doing philosophy in the West denies the face-to-face reality in which we—philosophers included—interact with persons different from ourselves. He argues that this "face-to-face" realm is not the same thing as the realm of abstract concepts. It possesses its own texture which is primarily an ethical one. In this domain we are challenged by "the otherness of the other person."

It is this "otherness," which is an integral characteristic of human life, but the Western philosophical tradition has overlooked and even negated it, thus contributing to the dehumanization of Man. Lévinas' life and thinking were deeply affected by the trauma of the Nazi genocide, better known as the Holocaust. But what is unique about his thinking is that it refuses to make those monstrous events its core subject matter. As Derrida, who admired Lévinas' philosophy, aptly expressed it once: the danger of naming our monstrosities is that they become our pets. Lévinas' writings provide no extensive discussion of the Holocaust itself; therefore, the assumption, on the part of those who were thinking and writing on it, has often been that Lévinas could not be considered a valid source of philosophical insight into this dark period of human history. But that is an erroneous assumption, just as invalid as the assumption that he unreservedly admired Heidegger's philosophy because he happened to have translated it into French. As a matter of fact, Lévinas' thinking is a reaction to the Holocaust by the mere fact that it asks the crucial question: What does it mean to be a human being? Were one to encapsulate the whole of Lévinas' philosophy in two succinct words, they would be "being human." This philosophy insists throughout that an extreme, unbalanced rationality devoid of imagination, feelings, senses and spirit, unconcerned with the ethical dimensions of life, is the equivalent to a refusal to be human, to allowing oneself to become a monster.

Not unlike Vico in the 18th century, he individuates such a root in the Cartesian ego, an autonomous center of consciousness which in modern philosophy has assumed the function of a paradigm for thinking about human beings. Lévinas does not deny this world-constituting ego, rather he leads it to the discovery of an ethical core within itself; which is to say, he uncovers another root growing within the first root which he calls the "self." The conundrum seems to be this: if it is true that the ego does the conceptual work of philosophy by announcing what there really is in the world, how can this ego then acknowledge the essentially ethical "self" which lives within itself? Somehow a bridge has to be found between this limitless power and freedom of the independent intellect, and the particular concrete ethical obligations to another person. For, this ethical self, unlike the ego, finds itself caught up with the welfare of the other prior to a conscious, rational decision, in a recognition, even when unwilled, of his/her humanity. Indeed this ethical capacity seems to come from another place than our rational powers of analysis evidenced within the Cartesian ego. Even if we grant that such an ego is adequate in identifying the truths of philosophy, it somehow remains unable to acknowledge a domain where there is no choosing of the connection with the other; in fact the other way around may apply: the other chooses me, one is "already responsible" for the other prior to any rational analysis.

And here is the philosophical paradox: Lévinas' task becomes that of using rationality to take the Cartesian ego beyond rationality, somewhat similar to what Vico does with his concepts of fantasia, which for him precedes rational reason, and the concept of Providence who guides human events and is both immanent within history but also transcendent. Which is to say, the rational ego has to be brought to recognize a sort of enigmatic "ethical" truth which Lévinas calls "pre-originary," i.e., arising outside, prior to the usual time-line of the reflective ego. In attempting this operation, Lévinas will proffer statements such as: ethics is "older" than philosophy, it is "first philosophy," on the scene before the arrival of rational philosophical thinking; something ingrained in being human. Within purely classical categories, that may be equivalent to the Socratic preoccupation with dying well by living a life of integrity and devotion to truth, as exemplified in Plato's Apology. It is this ancient voice of goodness, which even Vico's pre-historical "bestioni" possess to a degree, a voice often overlooked by rationalist philosophers, but powerfully present in Talmudic texts, that Lévinas finds strangely silent in the modern Western philosophical tradition.

In mytho-poetic language, it's as if Lévinas were to come face-to-face with the goddess Europa, as she is being abducted by a black bull (Zeus in disguise), to journey to another shore, there to assume a different persona, and he were to ask her, "Europa quo vadis?" after warning her to remember her original identity: "nosce te ipsum"; which is to say, go back to the future and know yourself holistically: know your Greco-Roman origins, yes, but also the Biblical tradition (the foundation for Christianity), the Christian heritage, the Humanistic synthesis of Graeco-Roman and Christian civilizations, Celtic and Germanic cultures with their ideas of freedom, the universalizing Enlightenment rooted in the democratic-scientific tradition born in ancient Greece, the Islamic influences. Voltaire and Descartes yes, but Vico and Novalis too are part of your identity. Your unity will be a chimera if it is only a unity of a bank and neglects its spiritual elements. Undoubtedly this hermeneutics, or re-interpretation of the Cartesian ego, placing at its core an non-refusable responsibility for the other without granting the ego any time to think it over and choose, so to speak, challenges some of the most basic assumptions of modern, and in some way classical, rationalistic philosophy.

Not since the times of Maimonides in the 13th century had a Jew dared such a fundamental challenge from within the Western philosophical tradition. It is the challenge of Paul to Greek culture revisited. For indeed Lévinas is saying nothing short of this: the knowing ego does not exhaust what it means to be human. Some have called his philosophy one of "ethical subjectivity," as a way of dismissing it as the raving of a lunatic, just as the ancient Greeks dismissed Paul in the agora. For the serious reader, however, it is rather a re-definition of subjectivity face to face with a totalizing kind of Cartesian reflection.

While Lévinas does not write directly about the Holocaust, other thinkers, who influenced Lévinas, were nevertheless reflecting upon the philosophical implications of this dark event of human history. One such was Berel Lang who wrote an essay titled "Genocide and Kant's Enlightenment," which appeared in his Act and Idea in the Nazi Genocide. In this essay Lang uncovers certain lines of affinity between some classical aspects of Enlightenment thought, and the Nazi genocide. His conclusion is that there are two important aspects of the Enlightenment that formed the intellectual heritage, which needed to be in place, for genocide to occur in the heart of civilized Europe: namely, the universalization of rational ideals, and the redefinition of the individual human being in terms of its possessing or not such a universal rationality. The genocide, Lang argues, was aimed at those groups who stuck to their own ancient pre-Enlightenment sources of particularistic identity, considered "irrational."

Hence the racial laws and racial exclusion were expression of ingrained Enlightenment prejudices. Which is to say, the Enlightenment sheds light on everything except itself; it remains to be enlightened. This powerful essay leads many cultural anthropologists comparing civilizations, to begin to wonder: which, in the final analysis, is more obscurantist: religious fanaticism and fundamentalism, or a so called "enlightened" era throwing out the window the baby with the bathwater and arrogantly refusing any suggestion that it ought to enlighten itself, and not with its own light?

This line of thought conjures up that terrible face to face encounter of Dante with the poet Bertrand Del Bornio in a cave in hell doing "light to himself" with its own decapitated head. There we have reason eating its own tail; internal logical thinking and assuming the grammar of lunacy. I dare say that such a question has not been satisfactorily answered yet. In that question lies the challenge of Lévinas' philosophy: in its displacing of the centrality of Cartesian thinking within modernity, in order to re-center it around ethics: the face-to-face encounter with another human being which is always hopeful unless it occurs in hell. Everything we have discussed above begs this particular question: is Lévinas' challenge to the Western philosophical tradition philosophically tenable? To answer the question adequately we need to be first aware that Emmanuel Lévinas, as well as Hermann Cohen and Franz Rosenweig (the author of *Echoes from the Holocaust: Philosophical Reflections in a Dark Time*, 1988), are representative of learned European Jews with great familiarity with the texts of both the Jewish and the Western philosophical tradition. They challenge the latter exactly because they are so knowledgeable in both.

Lévinas is fully capable of confronting the intellectual traps of those rationalists who would relegate him to the sphere of theology. To the contrary, he insisted on writing in both spheres and claimed that Jewish religious textuality contains hitherto unexplored philosophical insights. For this is a tradition which puts great emphasis on interpersonal, social and familial relationships; phenomena not contemplated in traditional Western philosophy. Which is to say, the challenge is to Western philosophy's totalizing pretense, beginning with Plato's times, that it can gather everything up in one synchronic whole. It is that challenge that irritates control freaks, thought policemen, rationalists and mysologists galore. It goes a long way in explaining their attempt to relegate Lévinas' philosophy to the sphere of the merely mystical.

Finally, let us briefly examine how Lévinas develops this fundamental challenge to Western rationalism. He names both the texts of Jewish tradition and philosophical discourse "the said," while calling the living activity of interpretative struggle (its hermeneutics) with the texts, and the self which suffers for the other, "the saying." The said always tries to capture the saying, which may partly explain the ancient grudge of Plato towards poets (see Plato's Republic, book X, on Homer). In any case, it is the saying which launches the said and puts it into circulation. The saying echoes outside of space and time destabilizing the comfortable, rationally secure positions rationalists take up in the said, in conceptual truths (thought to be universal and eternal), in a secure totalizing kind of knowledge. Yet it is this very destabilizing process that injects the ethical outward-directness into the said.

Lévinas will often contrasts the saying's vulnerable openness to the other (which he calls "being ex-posed) with the said's relative security (which he calls "exposition"). He asserts moreover, that there is a rich unexplored relationship between the way we are "exposed" in ethics, and the life "exposition" we use to analyze and order the world. Indeed, this is a new, essentially Jewish, philosophical reflection which places into question the claim to totalizing completeness, by an appeal to the priority of ethics. It insists that any person that confronts me, needs to be placed outside the totalizing categories seeking to reduce her/him to an aspect of a rational system. Basically, what Lévinas is doing is relocating our dangerous ability to deny others their legitimate sphere of difference; an ability which is capable of destroying our own humanity. This is nothing short than the core struggle for the achievement of moral humanity which was also the root ethical aim of Vico's *New Science*.

Like Vico, Lévinas shows us the way to keep the benefits of universal Enlightenment ethics while avoiding its perils. For, his ethics is not based on a totalizing sort of universalism, but on the particular concrete needs and demands of each unique individual, every "other' that I meet within time and space. Every time I meet the other, she/he constitutes an ethical challenge to my self, a challenge as to who I am as a human being. This kind of philosophy is a challenge to each one of us to go beyond nostalgic returns to Greek classicism, as important at that may be, in the understanding of Western Civilization; to establish intellectual-background-assumptions which are different from those of the Enlightenment; to search for urgently needed new cultural paradigms, new ways of thinking appealing to the priority of ethics and the importance of the particular as a category of thought, a place in thought wherein genocide and hatred of the other becomes inconceivable; in short to prepare new wineskins for the new wine which is a "Novantiqua Europa."

IV

In 1932 Christopher Dawson published a book titled *The Making of Europe* which had enormous success and established his reputation as a scholar of incredible range and erudition who could communicate with great clarity and elegance. He had previously written two other books: *The Age of the Gods* (1928), and *Progress and Religion* (1929), but this one was unique. The book avoids the conventional burdensome footnotes, bibliographies and theoretical frameworks and reads like a romantic novel, hence its popularity. Indeed, 19th century Romanticism was a corrective to the previous century, the so called age of Enlightenment. It did this by questioning the rationalist conviction that the empirical physical sciences constituted the paradigm of all knowledge and thus reinstated Giambattista Vico's revaluation of history against the Cartesian depreciation of it as mere gossip.

Vico had observed that the external world of nature is ultimately impenetrable, for the human mind can only attempt to manipulate it within the strict limits set by God who created it. The stream of history, on the other hand, is essentially the world that the human creative spirit has made, and therefore despite its recurring mysteries, it can come to be known by humans in an incomparably deeper sense. Dawson shared this revaluation of history as did Hegel when he declared history the highest form of knowledge: the self-realization of the absolute spirit in time. And what was the single idea, the keynote of Dawson's thought as found in The Making of Europe? I was this: religion is the soul of a culture and a society that has lost its spiritual roots is a dying society, however prosperous it may appear externally. The fate of our civilization was endangered not only by the fading of the vision of faith that originally formed it, namely Christianity, but the failure to integrate the world of reason and science with the world of the soul, which has lost the power to express itself through culture.

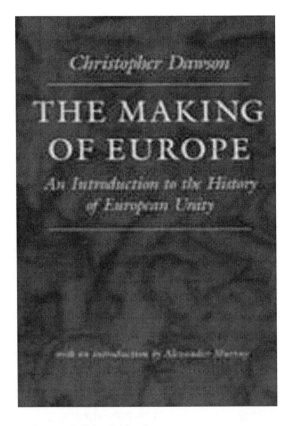

Figure 6.13. Dawson's most influential book.

In Dawson's view this was the tragedy of modern man. Before writing his famous book Dawson had read and pondered deeply the works of

Augustine (*The City of God*) and Edward Gibbon (*The Decline and Fall of the Roman Empire*). He was also influenced by Lord Acton's World History wherein Acton affirms that "religion is the key of history." He slowly became aware of the continuity of history and of how the coming of Christianity had transformed the dying Roman Empire into a new world. He spent fourteen years of intensive study before writing his twenty some books, among which *Enquiries into Religion and Culture (*1934*), Religion and Culture*(1948), *Religion and the Rise of Western Culture* (1950), *The Crisis of Western Education* (1961), *The Formation of Christendom* (1961). All these books dealt with the life of civilizations. The underlying idea in them was the interaction of religion with culture and subsequently with civilization.

Religion is discovered to be the dynamic element in every culture—its life and soul. He discovered that worship, prayer, the rite of sacrifice, and the moral law were common to all religions and so what the object of worship, and that moreover, the destiny of the human race was conditioned not only by material progress but by a divine purpose or providence working through history. Dawson also discovered that "the world religions have been the keystones of the world cultures, so that when they are removed the arch falls and the building is destroyed" (Progress and Religion, p. 140).

As he surveys the two millennia of Christianity Dawson noted four landmarks. The first one is the new element which defines the difference between the new faith and the old mystery religions of Europe: this is the principle of a dynamic and creative spirit that inspires the whole of life. The Christian religion has a power of renewal that has accompanied it through the ages. The second landmark was the extraordinary development in the fourth century A.D. when Constantine declared Christianity the official religion of the Roman Empire. After centuries of living on the inherited capital of the Hellenistic culture, this fountainhead seemed to run dry. Yet the achievement of Greece and Rome were not rejected by this new faith. They were merely transformed. Classical learning and the Latin language became fused with the ideals of a Christian society that was founded not on wealth, tyranny and power but on freedom, progress, and social justice. Latin became "not only a perfect vehicle for the expression of thought but also an ark which carried the seed of Hellenic culture through the deluge of barbarism" (The Making of Europe, p. 49).

The third great change of thought, according to Dawson, came about in the 16th century with the Renaissance and the Reformation, which brought an end to medieval unity. The fourth came about after the industrial revolution in the 19th century and led to the 20th century. In one of his last books Dawson, the Crisis of Western Education Dawson calls our own era the age of Frankenstein, "the hero who creates a mechanical monster and then found it had got out of control and threatened his own existence" (p. 189).He had in mind atomic warfare and he argued that if Western society were to gain control over these forces there would have to be a reintegration of faith and culture, and that there is an absolute limit to the progress that can be achieved by perfecting scientific techniques detached from spiritual aims and moral values. This is similar to Einstein's assessment of our era as one characterized by perfection of means and confusion of goals.

But let us go back to The Making of Europe which remains Dawson's best-known book. In it he demonstrates that Christianity has been the spiritual force that created the unity of Western culture, indeed the commonwealth of Europe itself, from the chaotic world of myriad warring tribes. He shows in that book how the Dark Ages, the period between 400 and 1000 A.D., became a dawn witnessing to the conversion of the West, the foundation of Western civilization and the creation of Christian art and liturgy. And he then asked a crucial question: If such a transformation could happen in the age of the barbarians could it not be repeated now?

Like the founding fathers of the EU Dawson, after the Second World War was already envisioning a new united Europe. But he soon realized that there was a problem which faced not only Europe but America too and all societies that consider themselves Western. The problem was this: the disastrous separation of culture from its religious base brought about by the modern barbarians of the mind and assorted nihilists had not been stemmed by the modern educational system which considered the study of religion superfluous and in fact aimed at its liquidation. The unity of thought, which had prevailed in European civilization over a thousand years, was shattered by excessive specialization which allowed the educated elites to see the tree while missing the forest; moreover science, philosophy and theology had long since split apart.

Education, rather than being a preparation for life, had become purely utilitarian and vocational. Humanistic studies needed to be resurrected in all schools and not preserved, almost as a relic of the past, in places like Harvard, Yale and Princeton Universities as a sort of frosting on the cake of education. This was urgent since the neo-barbarians had already entered the citadel of learning and were hard at work to destroy it from the inside.

Humanism as integrated with Catholicism was at the forefront of Dawson's speculation. It was that humanism which produced the medieval unity of the 13th century exemplifying Christian culture par excellence. For the flowering of art in every form reached its zenith in Europe between the 13the and 15th centuries with the poetry of Dante and Petrarch, the fresco painters of the Florentine school Giotto and Fra Angelico, and the sculptures of Michelangelo. It was also the age of saints and mystics, both men and women: St. Francis of Assisi, St. Dominick, St. Catherine of Siena, Julian of Norwich, Hildegard of Bingen, just to name a few.

It must also be mentioned that Dawson was not advocating a return to the Middle Ages; neither was he commending the external apparatus of medievalism, nor Charlemagne's so called Holy Roman Empire, but rather "a return to the forgotten world of spiritual reality" to which these centuries bear witness. He was not recommending a nostalgic evasion of the present day cultural dilemmas. He was indeed an intellectual for whom ideas were important, but many of his colleagues noticed a paradox in him: together with the remote facts of history, he knew of the latest current events in remote corners of the world, and understood and spoke several European languages.

Figure 6.14. The Annunciation by Fra Angelico.

Indeed, Dawson had the gift of seeing deeper and further than many of his contemporaries because he had the capacity to interpret the present in the light of the events of the past. As he put it: "The more we know of the past, the freer we are to choose the way we will go." To conclude, it is a mistake to think of Dawson as an anti-modern. Rather, what he was advocating was a retrieval of spiritual values in a godless and nihilistic world.

The reason he was assigned the first Chair of Roman Catholic Studies at Harvard University was that he had the reputation of being a very broadminded scholar, able to contemplate opposite ideas and integrate them. He was in short a consummate humanist who understood the universal character of the Church, a Church which belongs neither to East nor to West but stands as a mediator between the two. It was in fact his humanism which led him to conversion to Catholicism as it also happened for G.K. Chesterton, Graham Greene and David Jones. His was a beautiful mind.

V

There is a taken for granted theory on the part of Western intelligentsia that secularization is the inevitable result of modernization. Secularization is a particularly European experience. As strange and paradoxical as it may sound to European ears, that, despite differences between religious America and secular Europe, in the global future it will be entirely "normal" to be more fully modern and more fully religious at the same time. In fact, a dialogue between world religions remains an urgent and necessary cultural task of our times.

There are important implications for foreign policies and western attitudes towards Islamic countries still embedded, unfortunately, by the Voltairian anti-religion virus. It all comes together in Europe in the question of Turkey and this secular paradox as stated by the sociologist Josè Casanova: "In the name of freedom, individual autonomy, tolerance and cultural pluralism, religious people (Christian, Jewish and Muslim) are being asked to keep their religious beliefs, identities and norms 'private' so that they do not disturb the project of a modern, secular, enlightened Europe" The future reality is that religious people cannot and will not do this as we learn to live in a post-secular society.

Figure 6.15. Voltaire.

It appears that such a scenario will result in a post-secular Europe. This view is also held by none other than one of the most authoritative philosophers of contemporary Europe, Jurgen Habermas. Among other things he asks this pointed question originally asked in the *Journal of Philosophy* (2006:: 14: 1-25): *"Are religious issues simply to be regarded as relics of a pre-modern era, or is it the duty of the more secular citizens to overcome his or her narrowly secularist consciousness in order to engage with religion in terms of 'reasonably expected disagreement'?"*

Figure 6.16. A Romansque cathedral in Bitonto, Puglia.

Habermas addresses the debate in terms of John Rawls's concept of "public use of reason" and proposes that secular citizens in Europe learn to live, and the sooner the better, in a post-secular society; in so doing they will be following the example of religious citizens, who have already come to terms with the ethical expectations of democratic citizenship. So far secular citizens have not been expected to make a similar effort.

Eight Scholars' Views ... 83

Figure 6.17. Habermas' critique of the EU.

He is not alone in that challenge. In the year 2000 an essay came out written by Shmuel Eisenstadt, an Israeli sociologist, titled "Multiple Modernties (see *Daedalus* 129: 1-30) which right from its outset challenged the taken for granted assumption that modernizing societies are convergent, as well as the notion that Europe is the lead society in that converging modernizing process.

What the concept of multiple modernities implies is that Western (especially European) modernity is *not* the only conceivable one. It can come with indigenous differences. It would be enough to consider India, the largest democracy on earth which enshrines religion as part of its heritage and cultural patrimony. If one takes a careful look at the world outside the West one immediately notices that it is religion which defines the aspiration to an alternate modernity. That may well surprise the "enlightened" European mind, but there is such a thing as a Russian modernity inspired by Russian Orthodoxy, an Islamic modernity, a Hindu modernity, and what may surprise them even more, an integrally Catholic modernity. That was pointed out by Professor JHH Weiler whom we will examine further down. Those modernties are not illusions, as the old classical secularization theory tended to imply.

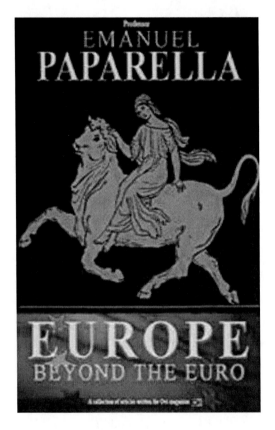

Figure 6.18. Paparella's critique of the EU.

Eisenstadt argues that modernity in its multiple dimensions is a continual mechanism of reappropriations and reinterpretations of the idea of modernity. Driven by individual socio-cultural influences brought about by globalization, emerging versions of modernity negotiate and create their spaces within a modern institutional framework. Given the dynamics of a continual diversification of multiple modernities, Eisenstadt concludes that neither of the Western-centric assumption of the 'end of history' or the 'clash of civilizations' hold true by the change of the century.

Perhaps the greatest surprise of all might be that, as hinted above, that in many parts of the world the West is perceived in a pejorative way, as propagating a decadent, hedonistic culture of irreligious materialism. Such a perception is reinforced by both the influence of intellectuals, usually heavily secular, and the omnipresence of the Western mass media, much of whose content can indeed be defined as materialistic and irreligious. If that be true, it ought to be of great interest to the practice of diplomacy of Western democracies. At the very least, this crucial question ought to be asked and discussed: What are the consequences of taking seriously the empirical sociological fact that for the great majority of the world's populations in the 21st century, it is not only possible, but quite normal to be both modern and religious? Might this question make a difference in the kind of paradigm that we construct in the West to better understand the nature of the modern world, be it European, American, Asian or African? Is it really "enlightened," as the age of Enlightenment surely supposed in Europe, to isolate the vast field of the sociology of religion, or should it be restored to its rightful place in the overall global social agenda? Which is to say, is the Enlightenment still to enlighten itself?

Besides Habermas, there is also an eminent American voice expressing the same ideas regarding a post-secular Europe. I refer to Professor JHH Weiler of New York University. In his article *"A Christian Europe? Europe and Christianity: Rules of Commitment"* first published in Italy as *"Un'Europa Cristiana,"* professor Weiler, who has studied the process of European integration for more than twenty-five years, speaks of a European Christian ghetto. Such a provocative statement is of course a mere metaphor rooted in a sad reality used purposefully by Dr. Weiler to jolt people out of their complacency. It should also be prefaced at the outset that Professor Weiler is neither a Christian nor a Catholic but a practicing Jew. This is important because in his knowledge of the history of the Church and its importance for the EU's identity he puts many Christians to shame.

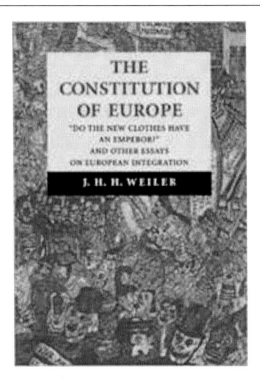

Figure 6.19. Weiler's critique of the EU.

Weiler writes that the manifestations of the external walls of this ghetto are very much in evidence in the refusal to include in the Preamble to the European Union Charter of Rights even a modest reference to Europe's religious heritage, completely ignoring the request of the former Pope John Paul II. In the recent draft Constitution there is still no reference to Europe's Christian heritage–but a generic allusion to its religious inheritance tucked between the cultural and the humanist!

What exactly does Dr. Weiler mean by the internal walls of the European Christian ghetto? The reason he calls them "internal" is that these are walls created by Christians themselves. This fact for Weiler is even more striking than the refusal of the EU Constitutional Conventions to make an explicit reference to Christianity. He points out that despite the explicit Catholic orientation of the founding fathers of the European construct, there isn't one major work, in any language, that explores in depth the Christian heritage and the Christian meaning of European integration. While writing his article Weiler pulled out from the library of his university 79 books published in the previous three years on the general phenomenon of European integration. None of them had a single allusion in the index to Christianity and its values. Weiler then writes that we ought not be too surprised that the Convention failed to make a reference to the Christian heritage of European integration, given that the Christian heritage has not been proclaimed, explored, debated, and made an integral part of the discourse of European integration by Christian scholars themselves.

This is puzzling indeed. Weiler has three possible explanations for the phenomenon. The first is a puzzling internalization of the false philosophical and constitutional premise of the most extreme forms of laicitÈ (secularity) as practiced for example in France. Freedom of religion is of course guaranteed and rightly so is also freedom from religious coercion. But on top of that there is the steadfast conviction that there can be no allusion or reference to religion in the official public space of the State, that such allusions are considered a transgression. A transgression of what exactly, we may ask.

There is the naive belief that for the State to be assiduously secular it needs to practice religious neutrality. Weiler considers this false on two counts: first, there is no neutral position in a binary option. For the State to abstain from any religious symbolism is no more neutral than for the state to espouse some forms of religious symbolism. The religiosity of large segments of the population and the religious dimension of the culture are objective data. Denying these facts simply means favoring one worldview over the other, masking it as neutrality.

The second explanation is that to accept that view of the relationship between State and religion is also to accept a secular (basically 18th-century) definition of what religion in general and Christianity in particular are. It is a vision that derives from the culture of rights which treats religion as a private matter by equating freedom of religion with freedom of speech, of belief, and of association. But then Weiler asks this crucial question: can one accept that Christianity be consigned to the realm of the private by the secular authorities of the State? That question is not to imply that Weiler does not believe in the liberal constitutional order with its guarantees of democracy and freedom. He does indeed, but he also believes in a vigorous and articulate religious voice and viewpoint in the public spaces guaranteed by constitutional democracies.

Figure 6.20. Abraham, the father of faith.

The conundrum here boils down to this: many Catholic scholars have confused the public disciplines of constitutional democracy with a private discipline of religious silence in the public sphere. Worse than that, Christian scholars have internalized the notion that to integrate Christian thinking and Christian teaching into their reflections on constitutional law, on political theory, on social science, is a betrayal of their academic standing, of their objectivity, of their scientific credentials.

Another reason adduced by Weiler is fear. Fear that in an academy dominated by an intellectual class which often leans to the left or to the center-left and insists on "politically correct" principles, an incorporation of Christian insight (other than a study in scientific fashion of religious phenomena) would brand the scholar as lacking in scientific objectivity; of not being a "free thinker." And finally Weiler mentions sheer ignorance. Precious few in the intellectual classes have read, studied, and reflected on the teachings of the Church, even less those of the current pontificate, its encyclicals, the apostolic letters, etc, with the same assiduousness that they study the latest offering from the secular intellectual icons of our generation.

Weiler maintains that while it is shocking that the explicit request of the Holy Father would be denied by the Convention, it is even more shocking that the call of this pontiff to the laity to be the messengers of Christian teaching in their own private and professional lives goes in many cases equally unheeded. The lives of those touched by faith cannot, once they exit the sphere of home and family, become identical with those not touched by faith. This is true for the shopkeeper in the market, for the conductor on the train, for a minister of the republic, as well as for those whose work is, in one way or another, a reflection on the public policies of public authorities.

One is led by the above reflections to inquire as to what is the relevance of Christianity and Christian teaching to the narrative of European integration. Weiler finds it laughable not to recognize Christianity as being a hugely important element in defining what we mean by European identity–for good and for bad. In art and in literature, in music and in sculpture, even in our political culture, Christianity has been a leitmotif–an inspiration as well as an object of rebellion. There is no normalcy within secularism in affirming this empirical fact; there is only normalcy in denying it. Weiler goes on to explain that while Christianity is a sociological and historical phenomenon, it is also a living faith based on revealed truth. Here is where Christian teaching becomes relevant.

The reader may now ask: what has all of this got to do with European integration? Weiler, speaking as a scholar and not merely as a believer, insists that indeed a great deal is at stake, that the narratives of history such as the story of European integration have no inherent meaning. They have the meaning we give them. What is at stake is what meaning we want to give. A Christian Europe is not a Europe that will endorse Christianity. It is not a call for evangelization. A Christian Europe is one that can learn from the teaching of Christianity. To reflect, discuss, debate, and ultimately assign meaning to European integration without reference to such an important source is to impoverish Europe. For lay people and for non-Christians, this becomes a challenge to match. Christianity today offers interesting "takes" on the central issues, the core issues, the deepest challenges in the very self-understanding of what Europe is about but few, even among Christians, are aware of it.

Weiler offers some examples which he hopes will motivate the reader to read and reflect on those teachings: the relationship to the "other"– within our society, across our boundaries within Europe, and beyond Europe–is arguably the most important challenge to which European integration tries to respond. Well, the encyclical *Redemptoris Missio* is a profound statement on how to think, to conceptualize a respectful relationship with the other. The Catholic teachings expressed in this encyclical are concerned with tolerance, respect, and inclusion, concepts inextricably connected with freedom and democracy. On the one hand, the encyclical bravely eschews the epistemological and moral relativism of post-modernity by affirming that which it considers to be the truth. But at the same time, it treats with the utmost respect those who do not share in that Truth. One cannot truly respect the other if one does not have respect for oneself, individually and collectively. Forgetting one's heritage is indeed a shabby mode of respecting oneself individually and collectively. Much can flow from this insight in the various debates on European integration.

For Dr. Weiler, the marketplace is another core issue of the European Union. Some would even argue that it is *the* core issue. Here again, Weiler points out that the encyclical *Centesimus Annus* offers one of the most profound reflections on the virtues of a free market but also of its dangers to human dignity. It is a reflection that goes well beyond the mantra of "solidarity" so dear to political activists of many stripes and which one finds endlessly in the debate of European integration. Europe need not espouse the teachings of the Church in this matter. But why exclude them from the debate? And there are many other examples in the book.

And of course the logical last inquiry is this: how would non-Christians react to the notion of a Christian Europe? Are we to exclude Turkey for example? Professor Weiler explains that a Christian Europe does not mean a Europe for Christians. It does not mean an official endorsement of, or call for, evangelization. That is certainly not the role of the European Union. It simply means a Europe that does not deny its Christian inheritance and the richness that public debate can gain from engagement with Christian teachings.

Weiler points out that there is something comic bordering on the tragic in observing those most opposed to any reference to religion or Christianity in the draft Constitution at the forefront of opposition to Turkish membership in the Union. It is indeed an insult to Christianity and its teaching of grace and tolerance to claim that there is no place in Europe for a non-Christian country or worse, for non-Christian individuals. Weiler underlies the fact that he is an observant Jew, the son of a rabbi with European roots that go back hundreds of years and that his ancestors were often the victims of Christians and Christianity; yet he finds it puzzling that anyone would fear the recognition and acknowledgment of the dominant culture (i.e., Christianity) as an empirical historical fact, and reveals a fear of his which is also an insight, and it is this: "If I have a fear, it is the following: to deny the relevance of the Christian heritage in European public symbolism and European public space, for to deny that is to deny, too, the relevance of my own religiosity in that same public space." That would probably be just fine for those who wish to eliminate religion altogether from both the public and the private sphere, but it remains a shortsighted social and political strategy, for if a body politic is based on the rejection of one's history and heritage, it will be built on sand and will ultimately not survive. We may have seen the beginning of this unraveling in the EU in June 2016. Time will tell.

Essay 7

THE CORRUPTION OF RELIGION: RUSSIA'S MILITARY-ECCLESIASTICAL COMPLEX

"Putin is planting Russia's flag firmly on the side of traditional Christianity"
                                                                                --Pat Buchanan

Figure 7.1. Leviathan.

In the recent award winning movie "Leviathan" by Andrei Avyagintsev we observe the white skeleton of a beached whale. In the foreground there is a man gazing over it. In the background one notices a squalid coastal town in Russia's frigid north, the port of Pribrezhny. The beauty and majesty of the whale's skeleton stands in stark contrast to the ugliness of the town where men go about their business obsessively and hypocritically searching for their daily share of power and greed, all fittingly recreated in the film, a great film concerned with the corruption of religion.

One immediately suspects that in this film we have much more than meets the eye. A theological-literary hermeneutics is needed. The title "leviathan" alone would suggest it. It literally means big whale but it also suggests majesty and awesome power, as Thomas Hobbes famously hinted at in his famous political tract "Leviathan" alluding to the awesome power of the modern state. So "leviathan" is a highly charged symbolical term. One can easily go back to its Biblical connotations and draw on both the Book of Job and the story of Naboth's Vineyard, in which an evil king trumps up false charges to seize the belongings of a poor neighbor. The Biblical leviathan is mentioned on several occasions, sometimes as a seagoing animal, but also as a fearsome monster of evil, slain by God himself in cosmic warfare. In this apocalyptic vision, the image becomes "the piercing serpent."

Let's attempt to interpret those powerful Biblical symbols as shown in the film. Leviathan, or better, Leviathan's monstrous skeleton could be nothing less than the awesome aspirations of the old Soviet Union, assuming that those past times are some kind of lost glory. There is always nostalgia for lost glory, to wit the recent Brexit of the UK. What may be in play is a needed substitution of the language of Marxism-Leninism, back to that of Christianity. As Jung used to quip: throw religion out the window and it will come back the back door.

The Corruption of Religion

Figure 7.2. The Kremlin and St. Basil's Cathedral.

The plot of the story in the film focuses on Kolya, an auto mechanic who spends most of his life in a drunken haze. He owns a property that is coveted by the local mayor, Vadim, who gets everything he wants through the exercise of political power, to the point of deploying thugs to enforce his will. Ultimately, Kolya is loses his home. Vadim as a transparent stand-in for Vladimir Putin, who also rules through violence and extra-legal trickery. For both men, law is merely a tool for the powerful. If it sounds Machiavellian, it is.

Figure 7.3. State and church.

This is mere satire, but the uniqueness of the film resides in the fact that these banal events of an obscure Siberian town are set in a cosmic context, within Biblical symbolism. That is to say, modern Russians live in the shadow of the slain leviathan. No wonder that the Russian media have mostly ignored the film's great success! Surprisingly, that is not the case in the West (both in Europe and the US) where the film has received critical acclaim and has attracted the attention of far right reactionaries. How do we explain this paradox? Could it be that due to the film's political overtones, it is being used as an ideological propaganda tool?

Figure 7.4. Vladamir Putin.

Let's briefly explore this vexing question. It can only be answered adequately if we focus not only on Putin's criticism but on the Orthodox Church to which adhere some 250 million followers. Here is where the film is at its most daring. In the treatment of the town's orthodox bishop who serves as spiritual advisor to Vadim. In a Dostoyevsky-like scene, reminiscent of the Grand Inquisitor, the Bishop informs Vadim that despite the fact that all is in God's hands, God expects him to exercise to the fullest the power granted him in order to defeat the Enemy. As the story progresses we realize that one of the reason for stealing Koyla's property was the building of a brand new Orthodox cathedral inaugurated by the

Bishop with an eloquent sermon uniting Russian nationalism with the interests of the Orthodox Church marching under the glorious banner of truth and justice. Now, the bishop can easily be identified with Kirill, the Metropolitan of the Russian Orthodox Church who has involved the Church with an alliance with the post-Soviet regime. We need to remember here that support for authoritarian regimes is deeply embedded in Orthodox political thought tinged with a millenarian mystical nationalism. It would be enough to read Dostoyevsky's novels to realize as much. There Orthodox Russia is presented by its representatives as a bastion of true faith besieged by the immorality and false values of a secularized West.

The apocalyptic stage is set for Holy Russia confronting a Godless and decadent West. Putin himself has warned that "many Euro-Atlantic countries have moved away from their roots, including Christian values..." It couldn't be more clear. This Orthodox framing of Russian nationalism ensures that powerful Rightist groups willingly rally to Putin and his KGB clique. We in the West worry about Iran's theocracy with apocalyptic dreams abetted by nuclear weapons and yet we continue to ignore a state close to Iran where ambitious Machiavellian theocrats shape the national ideology of a regime which presently has at its disposal some 1,500 active nuclear weapons, and 8,000 of them in storage.

But not everyone ignores this bizarre phenomenon of the alliance of religion and nationalism. Historians of course know quite well that countries like Italy and Austria were considered Catholic countries and yet fought World War I on opposite sides. So nationalism within modernity has always trumped religion. This reality has now percolated to the not so educated of the likes of Trump who now appears on Russian TV, compliment of Larry King. The poorly educated and the political far right has also taken notice and has been absorbing the distorting caricature of Orthodox Christianity's spirituality through Putin's lenses.

It has percolated to the American ideological far right; to the likes of Pat Buchanan. Strangely enough, while during the Cold War he and his ilk vehemently railed against the Soviet Union as godless, now he has made an about face and branded the US as the new Evil Empire and has declared the new Cold War as a "war of beliefs," asking this revealing question:

"Whose side is God on now?" So, Russia is now the defender of Judeo-Christian values, as far as Buchanan is concerned. We are back to the Crusades and the War of religions, never mind the love and tolerance and compassion advocated by all genuine religion.

Figure 7.5. A Bible in one hand and a gun in the other.

Putin's and Buchanan vision, in which autocracy is married to Orthodox faith, may resemble somewhat the role that Franco's Spain occupied for decades, an authoritarian regime with which some conservative Catholic Americans sympathized because that regime resisted Communism, privileged the Catholic Church and upheld many aspects of Catholic moral teaching in public policy. While preferable to the Stalinists who tried to seize Spain in the 1930s, and although a Cold War ally to the U.S. very much unlike Putin's current strategic opposition, the Franco regime was a dictatorship that persecuted opposition and could not be a sustainable friend, much less role model, for most American Christians. It was certainly not democratic, nor tolerant, nor genuinely Christian. Idem for Putin's Russia.

Let me conclude by asserting that what we have in place today is not the true face of Orthodoxy which is rooted in the idea that "God is love," but a gigantic distortion via the faces of Putin and Buchanan. Some of those so called "Christians," alas, like Buchanan, consider themselves good Catholics but the God they worship is a tyrant, a la Putin, not the God of love which is celebrated whenever Pope Francis and the Patriarch Bartholomew get together, be it in Jerusalem or Greece or Rome. What obtains is the distortion and the corruption of religion reduced to an instrument of ideological policy.

Essay 8

CORRUPTION AND THE SELF-DESTRUCTION OF DEMOCRACY

"Hitler was first elected, and then he destroyed his people"

--Pope Francis

"America will never be destroyed from the outside. If we falter and lose our freedoms, it will be because we destroyed ourselves."

–Abraham Lincoln

The two above mentioned quotes in some way complement and explain each other. What the Pope is implying is what Lincoln prophesized; misguided people may vote for the monsters they have created and ultimately for their own downfall and destruction. The question arises: has Lincoln's prophecy been fulfilled with the election of Donald Trump? Are we in the process of destroying ourselves, just as it happened with the Roman Empire which began the process of moral self-destruction with the installment of deranged emperors such as Caligula or Nero?

Only five days after the inauguration on the 20th of January 2017, it has become apparent to any observant spectator that Trump has already recreated the corruption of Tammany Hall in the 1800s and early 1900 when cronyism dominated this nefarious group of New York politicians whose only aim was that of satisfying their personal ambitions through any actions, legal or illegal. That was especially true under Tweed in 1858 when corruption in the form of kickbacks from public works programs invaded practically every aspect of city and state governance.

Imperceptibly but inexorably democracy is being replaced by an oligarchy of corrupt politicians aiming at control of the people and putting profits before people. With the Trump presidency the US is now at risk of becoming a plutocracy catering to the rich, the only ones to enjoy the freedoms and rights guaranteed for all by the Constitution.

Figure 8.1. A plutocrat?

Trump has a shining example in Putin who has managed to become just about the richest man in Russia and whose net wealth is at least 10 times that of Trump. That may go a long way in explaining the affinity and admiration the two men feel for each other. The problem of course is that a plutocracy cannot exist without a fascist government equipped with a propaganda machine where the truth is what the government says it is and alternate facts can be dished out any time the government is scrutinized and criticized by the media.

On the day of his presidential inauguration, it was already clear how Donald Trump would govern. We've seen his Cabinet appointees, and

Corruption and the Self-Destruction of Democracy 103

watched some of their confirmation hearings and they are very revealing. Now we've got a first glimpse of his budget ideas. What they predict is a veritable orgy of conflicts of interest, looting and corruption ending in violation of the Constitution and an unmitigated disaster.

Trump has already instituted policies designed to repeal the first amendment. He has proudly declared that he has a running war with the press. And he made such declaration in front of the wall memorializing CIA members who died in their line of duty, blaming the press for his communication difficulties with the agency.

Some in the press are still deluding themselves with the notion that our constitutional provisions of checks and balances among the various branches of government will ultimately save the day and correct this abnormal situation. Others are not so sanguine and are afraid that we might have seen our last free election. Next time around the election will not only be rigged but will be decided before any voting occurs.

Let's examine Trump's budget plan first. During the campaign, he flirted with left-leaning fiscal ideas, saying he wouldn't cut Social Security and Medicare. But thus far he is going in the exact opposite direction, albeit his populism, as a way of deceiving the middle class which he has exploited and manipulated his whole life, remains strong.

Last year the Republican Study Committee came up with an ultra-conservative plan to slash federal spending by $8.6 trillion over 10 years. But Trump's initial budget has cuts of *$10.5 trillion*. The details aren't worked out yet, but it is becoming more and more obvious that that all manner of government agencies would be gored or killed off altogether and that foxes have been placed in charge of chicken coops. The Corporation for Public Broadcasting would be privatized, the National Endowment for the Arts and the National Endowment for the Humanities would be eliminated. They are considered unnecessary frosting on the cake. Barbaric times call for barbaric solutions. Several offices designed to help minorities would be gone. Research and scientific spending would be sharply rolled back and several agencies dedicated to climate change and renewable research would be simply abolished. Seventy five per cent of government environmental regulations are scheduled for elimination. Who needs a livable environment if we have jobs and economic prosperity. That too seems to be considered frosting on the cake.

The scale of these proposed cuts is simply staggering. The military, debt payments, Social Security, Medicare, and Medicaid account for three quarters of the federal budget. It is literally impossible to get that scale of cuts without cutting deeply into some of those programs. And when you dig into the budget proposed by the Heritage Foundation, which the Trump plan is based on, it turns out everything but defense is getting slashed — Social Security by 8 percent, Medicare by 41 percent, all domestic discretionary spending by 41 percent, and Medicaid by 47 percent. And with Republicans in charge of most state governments, huge austerity at the state level can also be expected.

The rationalization for these cuts is that they are about cutting the deficit, but in reality they are about making budget headroom for large tax cuts for the rich, the so called top 1 per centers. The outrageous lie is apparent by the choice of cabined officials; a good number of them are millionaires or billionaires, or people who have spent their careers undermining the very departments to which they have been appointed (Sessions, Perry, Puzder), and then there are those, like Tillerson who like Trump are clueless about the nature of public service, or De Vos who fits in all three categories.

Private industry will be in charge of the state and it will be called "business as usual." In the book *The Wrecking Crew* Thomas Frank elucidates how corruption is usually a logical product of a misguided approach to government. When the very idea of quality government is treated with scorn declaring government incompetent and inefficient, and the normative principles are greed, private industry, markets, to which all human society is subordinated, the predictable result is a Frankenstein monster who eventually turns around and destroys the very people who created it. But the worst turbulence, I am afraid, is still to come. Please buckle your seat-belts.

Essay 9

POPE FRANCIS'S URGENT WARNING ON THE DANGERS OF POPULISM

"Hitler didn't steal power, his people voted for him, and then he destroyed his people... Crisis provokes fear...that is the risk. In times of crisis we lack judgment."

–Pope Francis

Recently Pope Francis has drawn a startling parallel between the rise of populism on both sides of the Atlantic, with its leaders promising a restoration of national identity and wholeness (e.g., Le Pen, or Trump), and the rise of the Nazis some 80 years ago.

It's perhaps worth remembering here that almost a year ago he declared that "a person who thinks only about building walls, wherever they may be, and not building bridges, is not Christian." To that statement Trumped replied at the time that only a Trump administration could protect the Vatican from ISIS.

Basically, with the inauguration of a new avowedly populist US presidency, the Pope is now cautioning Europeans against the lure of populism parading as nationalism and patriotism which in the past has led to catastrophes such as World War II.

Some pundits have caustically observed that it was only a matter of time before the "Combed-Over Titan of Twitter, the con-artist of the Art of the Deal clashed with the Man in White." The collision was all but inevitable when one contrasts the two men: the celibate and the libertine, the mystic and the materialist, the humble and the vain, the ascetic and the ostentatious. But others have pointed out that, for all their differences as exhibited and fought over on the world stage, there are also puzzling similarities and affinities.

In the first place the two men are similar in their status as outsiders determined to shake up the establishment which they deem corrupt and uncaring of the people and the integrity of the institutions they lead. That is to say, they both exhibit a populist stance against elitism and privilege, although the case can certainly be made that one is genuine and the other is hypocritical and fake. But, in fact, most people do not bother with such subtle distinctions. They judge by appearances and alternate facts.

Alternate facts aside, it is undeniable that Trump has repeatedly attacked Republican elites and broken with Republican party orthodoxy on trade, foreign policy, campaign financing, conflict of interests, pretty much the same way that Francis has challenged the Vatican bureaucracy and traditional, settled Catholic doctrine fueled by the desire "to make a mess," as the Pope puts it, disregard the tired stale institutions, and start afresh.

Moreover, their rhetorical stratagems seem to mirror each other; they both have a fondness for name calling which is quite rare among popes and presidents. Trump resorts to "low energy," "liar," "crooked," "loser," while the Pope may resort to more theologically loaded epithets such as "Pharisee," or "self-absorbed Promethean neo-Pelagian" while occasionally also referring to "whiners," and "sourpusses." In any case, they both exhibit a skillful mastery of the contemporary media environment with its provocative unpredictability; an environment where the prevalent currency seems to be having people wonder in shock and amazement if "did he really just say that?" thus attracting immediate attention. It's the world of the blog and the twit, rather than that of the reflective essay. In some way, both men excel at salesmanship, albeit the Pope admittedly possesses much deeper intellectual ingenuity.

Both men seem to believe that a bit of troublemaking is the best way to attract attention with the discontented and the disaffected; which, come to think of it, is the essence of populism. Of course their constituencies differ: Trump speaks to the disaffected working middle class who has been feeling left out lately, never mind that the profits have all gone to the one per centers of the rich and glamorous to which Trump belongs. One way to cover that fact is with the alternate fact of rabid nationalism parading as patriotism. Pope Francis, on the other hand, as a Latin American and a globalist, speaks for the world's poor. That explains the stark difference in their immigration and refugee policies.

Nevertheless, they share a common enemy, not just those who advocate "business as usual" as Republicans or as Catholics, but the wider Western elitist ruling class. Both men promise deliverance from this opportunistic bureaucracy with its unresponsive and inconvenient institutions (such as regulatory offices) while emphasizing novelty and even whim. It is certainly a respite from the dry positivist approach of modern culture.

And this of course is populism's dilemma and peril: at times it relays not so much on the spirit of reform or renewal but on that of personal charisma, on a dangerous personality cult, what Nietzsche calls "charismatic man" ready to "trans-valuate values" in the quest of making America or the Catholic Church "great again." It is precisely what makes hese populist men and women interesting that can also make them unpredictable, even dangerous.

Essay 10

WHITE SUPREMACY IN THE WHITE HOUSE: ROOTED IN A DARK THEORY OF HISTORY

The Fourth Turning: What Cycles of History Tell Us about America's Next Rendezvous with Destiny b*y William Strauss and Neil Howe.*

The theoretical slogan "Make America Great Again," followed in practice with a ban on travel to the US from seven Moslem countries, is ultimately rooted in a sinister theory of history. The theory does not originate from the new occupant of the White House, who has never exhibited much intellectual curiosity or originality, be it in history, or any other subject for that matter, with the possible exception of shady business deals, but it is endemic to his most influential and trusted advisor Steve Bannon, the man behind the curtain who landed him in the White House.

Bannon is known as a White Supremacist, with racial and anti-Semitic tendencies; a passionate adherent to a theory of history about America's future as elucidated in the above mentioned book. There are around a plethora of cyclical theories of history, the most popular being perhaps that of the philosopher of history Giambattista Vico. One could indeed go all the way back to the ancient Greeks who believed that at the end of a given cycle of history (the saeculum) comes a "ekpsyrosis" or a cataclysmic event, a trial of fire of sorts, which destroys the old order and brings about a new one, but this new theory by Strauss and Howe is unique in its sheer darkness. To boot, Bannon misinterprets it to better suit his own political agenda.

As per this theory, there are three turning of history which America has experienced, so far: the Revolutionary War, the Civil War, the Great Depression followed by World War II. They were marked by massive dislocations, war, and decay from which the people were forced to reunite and build a new order. In other words, first comes a catalyst event from which issues a period of regeneracy climaxed by a war with the old order which ends with a resolution. The resolution is the triumph of the new order.

Bannon seems to be obsessed with the theory. He is convinced that a reckoning is fast approaching, in fact it must necessarily arrive in order for a new order to emerge; also, that the climactic conflict will be conducted from the White House. He has shown himself willing to advise Trump on the enactment of policies disruptive of the current order. It is generally believed that the he was the architect behind the ban, called temporary for now, on travel and on entry Muslims in the US. He was also behind the deletion of the reference to Jews as victims of the Holocaust on its recent yearly commemoration (on the very same day of the ban enacted on Moslems by executive fiat), never mind that Trump's son in law and daughters are practicing Jews.

One of the side-effects of this encouraged disruption is the breaking down of old political and economic alliances, even the turning away from traditional American principles to create chaos and prepare for the new order. Chaos seems to be the climate in the present White House: rampant confusion under conflicting orders, with Caligula redivivus creating the confusion and then perversely enjoying the reality show, to suddenly show up as the referee man with the brilliant solutions. It's as if the Apprentice TV show were still going on. It's the atmosphere of the Roman Colosseum where the phenomenon of survival of the fittest is the ultimate goal and rationale. Many, in and out of the White House, are concerned and are beginning to entertain the idea of impeachment. Some have even mustered the courage to call him "illegitimate," which is the equivalent to the little boy in Christian Andersen's tale shouting "the emperor is naked" as the emperor struts around in his splendid invisible clothes to the sycophantic admiration of his followers.

The bizarre show, as of this writing, goes on unabated. It has to go on, necessarily, because Bannon is attempting to bring about, even if for the moment he does it from outside the White House, or fulfill, if you will, the so called fourth turning of US history, a new vision of America as described in the theory above. Trump is merely the means to attain to it. In an interview Bannon has described Trump as "a blunt instrument" but one that he is perfectly willing to use nevertheless, in order to attain the appointed goal of history. It is all rather deterministic with human responsibility, guilt and regret, notably absent from the whole process.

Nevertheless, taking notice of this fourth turning gives some needed context to policies that so far seem deranged, incoherent and inconsistent, unexplainable and confusing even to experts in geo-politics, as they vainly attempt to square the circle and make some rational sense of it all.

Bannon is convinced that we are already in a period of regenaracy. The catalyst was the financial crisis of 2008. As described in the book, this is a period of isolationism, of reimagining the economy (which so far has shown itself prone to a reimagining new tax breaks for the rich...), rebuilding of the infrastructure, and, most importantly, a strong centralized, authoritarian, powerful government where the executive reigns supreme, unencumbered by too many laws and regulations. But this is only a preparation for a massive conflict of civilizations to come. A conflict between East and West, which may mean the Middle East or perhaps China. Russia, for the moment, seems to be considered a friendly ally, with few if any rationales.

Figure 10.1. Historical cycles or conspiracy theory?

But what does history ultimately show? Does it really repeat itself deterministically, or are the catastrophes of every era unique to each era? Will the fourth Turning be the same as the first, second, and third? To take a close look, it appears that the Fourth Turning of the Civil War was quite different than that of the Depression and World War II.

Logically, it is argued, the financial crisis of 2008 is the catalyst for our crisis and the coming struggle, just as the Depression was for the third turn. But are the two really comparable? During the Depression unemployment reached 20%; in the fourth turning it never went beyond 10%. Unlike the Hoover Administration (an administration which prided itself for its business acumen) which dilly dallied for two whole years, the government of Barack Obama acted very fast to prevent a meltdown and turned the situation around, at least on a financial level.

What this financial crisis has brought about this time around is an exacerbation of the income inequality gap which has been growing globally since it began some forty years ago. That explains the popularity of a Bernie Sanders, and to a certain extent that of Donald Trump, who as one of those who benefitted from and produced the gap, then skillfully used it as a campaign strategy to fool millions of middle class workers who are now waiting for the check in the mail. Good luck. The disappointed will be palpable in a few months.

Figure 10.2. The financial crisis as a sign of a clash of civilization?

If there is a comparison to be made, it ought to be that of the inaugural address of President Franklin Delano Roosevelt in 1933, when he describes a county devastated by the Great Depression, a picture that all Americans could see and recognize; and compare it to that of Trump in his inaugural address where he talks of a dark "American carnage." What was he talking about? He may not know himself, for Bannon was behind it. But it may aptly describe the deep divisions presently existing in this country of ours and what may be coming.

Unlike the era of FDR which put people back to work and created a national unifying spirit wherein society's resources were redistributed and society rebuilt, what is most apparent today is discord and disunity, as exemplified by the two main political parties who have all but forgotten the word compromise and harmony. The anger and the authoritarianism is there, apparent to all, but not the yearning for social justice, not the common purpose, or the common good. Division and dissension have been promoted as never before.

And this is where Bannon and his minions in the White House are greatly misguided. They believe that they are working for "the Gray Warrior," the leader described by Strauss and Howe who will "urgently resist the idea that a second consecutive generation might be denied the American Dream." The identification of the Gray Warrior in a pathological narcissist who creates "alternate facts" as he goes along is indeed a grevious mistake.

They also conveniently forget that the new order in the Germany of 1932 was inaugurated by a power-mad fellow named Adolf Hitler who wanted to make Germany great again. Pari passu, today's hero and savior, while claiming to be champion of the disadvantaged, continues to pursue his own personal financial and political interests and has so far shown precious little compassion for the poor and the unfortunate.

In reality, the ones who may eventually show us the way forward, out of our impasse and begin the Fourth Turning are not the Trumpists in love with Ayn Rand's "virtue of selfishness" but the Millennials, the young, whose needs have all but been ignored by the likes of Trump and Bannon.

The only candidate who attracted them during the presidential campaign was Bernie Sanders. Trump appealed and managed to fool mostly an older generation who felt that something had been taken away from them and resented that fact. The millennials have no such resentment; they have, in fact, never been given a chance at the American Dream in the first place. Most of them voted against Trump, many stayed home and for good reasons: Trump had offered them nothing.

What Bannon has failed to grasp is that the Fourth Turning, as envisioned by Strauss and Howe, is not inevitable and deterministic but requires an urgent return to a constitutionally agreed-upon set of values. The millennials have grasped that much. What Bannon and Trump are doing, on the other hand, is that, far from unifying against outside threats, they are creating enemies galore (Mexico, China, Australia, the EU, you name it) which many Americans don't want to have. That insistence on creating enemies at a tough bargaining table, does nothing but increase the palpable anxiety and frustration.

Figure 10.3. Steve Bannon contemplating the turns of history.

Indeed, we find ourselves in uncharted perilous territory and history cannot deterministically predict where we will eventually end up. It can only give us guidelines and lessons on how to avoid past mistakes. History however does teach us that to ignore the voices of justice and reason is to make sure that we will end up with an enormous political disaster on our hands. In a way we already have one reigning disaster right inside the White House. Those who did not vote for confusion and dissension (by a difference of 3 million votes) are now asked to go along for the ride with the mad emperor. Such are the ways and byways of democracy. In any case, better buckle up; the ride is likely to be bumpy.

Essay 11

POWER WITHOUT MORAL COMPASS: CALIGULA, TRUMP, PIUS XIII, AND MACHIAVELLI

Figure 11.1. The young Pope Pius XIII. A different kind of movie and Pope.

"Smoking is ok if the Pope does it"

-Pius XIII in "The Young Pope"

"If the President does it, it is not illegal"

-President Nixon during his impeachment

It is practically impossible to watch the latest rage on cable TV, the serial ten episode narration of a future Pope, Pius XIII, and not be struck by the uncanny parallels between it and the ancient political situation under emperor Caligula of the Roman Empire, as well as the present political landscape in the Atlantic Alliance under President Trump.

The movie is directed by Oscar winner Paolo Sorrentino, who knows well ancient Roman history and more recent Italian history, the Italy of Berlusconi, Pius X, Pius XII, as well as Hitler, Mussolini and other madmen of the times.

Critics have accused the film of being a caricature of the Papacy, a gossipy reality show of the Vatican who portrays an interesting character (the mad Pope) but not a real-to-life personality; a Vatican melodrama glittering with pomp and circumstances of the Vatican; but that is a misinterpretation, a superficial rendition of the content of the film,

Right from the first episode we are alerted that the real issue of the film is the issue of political power on which both Niccolo Machiavelli and Francis Bacon meditated so deeply. Machiavelli said that in politics "the end justifies the means." Francis Bacon said that "knowledge is power" and they said a mouthful. The ancient idea was that knowledge is virtue; now, within enlightened modernity knowledge is power to be seized and held at any cost.

The movie is, in fact, about the intricacies of power, temporal power, at the heart of Catholicism; something that has gone on now for some 17 centuries, since Constantine allegedly donated one third of Italy to the Pope thus creating the Papal temporal power and initiating the problematic mixing of the transcendent and the temporal within Christianity. Dante places three popes in hell because of that improper mixing.

The issue of power is perhaps the main idea explored in the series, and this right from the first episode where we witness this intriguing conversation between the newly elected young American Pope, Lenny, and the cardinal Secretary of State, his aide in the administration of the Vatican. During the conversation what comes through is that the new Pope has been elected by the cardinals because of his youth and inexperience in the intricacies of power which will render him easy to manipulate and control.

For the cardinals immersed in the Byzantine intrigues of the Vatican, good disciples of Machiavelli and Bacon that they are, power is knowledge and knowledge is power. During the conversation the Cardinal Secretary asks "Do you know why all the good souls of this world rage against power?" "Why, Your Eminence?" "Because they simply don't know what it is." "What is it?" "Power is knowledge." There you have it. That short exchange contains the key of the narrative: the issue of power, of power devoid of a moral compass.

Niccolo Machiavelli   Francis Bacon

Figure 11.2. Knowledge is power.

While the new pope understands the importance of knowledge in order to obtain and maintain power, he also understands it in a very instinctive emotional way. He feels that he is the Pope not because of his abilities, or his faith, or his compassion, but because it is his destiny. Power, as understood by the new Pope, trumps (pun intended) tradition, law, and even truth. When the Pope starts smoking in the papal palace we witness the following exchange: *"Holy Father, Holy Father, smoking is not allowed in the papal palace!" "Is that so? Who decided that?" "John Paul II." "The Pope?" "Yes, the Pope." "There's a new Pope now." "True."*

But why have the cardinals chosen an unbalanced sociopath? Well, they thought that he would be easy to manipulate, an easy to market moderate Pope, a rather naïve person, as most Americans supposedly are. They are to be greatly disappointed. Lenny is not your average Pope. What they got is Caligula redivivus who installs Sister Mary (Diane Keaton) as his closest advisor, violates the sanctity of the confessional (to get to the secrets by which he can blackmail, compromise and wield power over the cardinals), questions even the existence of God.

How can one not see the similarities between Caligula, the sociopathic emperor, Pius XIII, the sociopathic Pope, and Trump, the sociopathic President? They are all pathological narcissists; the universe revolves around them; they are gods, unpredictable, disdainful of common people in general, especially tourists. They like to see them humiliated. Moreover, have disdain for conventional moral principles. They all repudiate the tradition of their predecessors. The Pope wants to make the Catholic Church Great Again. If it sounds familiar, it is. In short Pius XIII is a version of Donald Trump. Both men, one in fiction one in reality (a reality show, if truth be told) have tapped into the wave of discontent sweeping the world which in turn has given rise to extreme right movements culminating in Brexit and the potential break-up of the Atlantic Alliance (NATO).

This Young Pope is so appealing not as a person that in fact does not exist at the moment, but because of his complex contradictions and his character. All narcissists and madmen are complex appealing characters, but not in any positive mode. At the start of the episodes the Pope defines himself as a contradiction: "I am a contradiction, like God." What is pathological is that he thinks of himself not as God's representative or witness on earth, but as a god, the way a Caligula did, the way a Trump does.

These people are compelling not because they are in any way admirable, but because we just can't stop talking about them. We keep asking in wonderment: why do people accept the bullying, why all that rudeness. Why the lack of challenge? Most importantly, what is it about power, about the bully culture of "might makes right" that turns people into monsters?

Figure 11.3. Chain smoking by "the young Pope".

Some tentative answers can be supplied by a comparison between Trump and the Young Pope. Like the Pope who says that smoking is OK in the Vatican palace if the Pope does it, (and nobody else), Trump seems to have gone back to the famous Nixon quip "if the President does it, it is not illegal." This is scary stuff for the survival of democracy. Both man lack a clear moral policy agenda for their institutions. What is clear is the Machiavellian goal of asserting power and making sure that nobody dares to challenge it. They are out to get what they want, no matter how petty. They rule by creating dissensions and confusion and establishing capricious priorities, like that of buying back the papal tiara from the basilica in Washington and wear it as he is carried about in the "sedia gestatoria," as a saint of heaven, a tradition long in disuse.

Power, shock and awe is the goal to be grasped as an end in itself and in whose name all means are acceptable. As the young Pope says: "Power is domination, control and therefore a very selective form of truth, which is a lie." One needs to create one's alternative facts to keep one's enemies down, humiliate them and destroy them. At the same time one needs to keep the people entertained with showmanship. Make them wonder, whom they are really dealing with; be ready to punish anyone who dares tell the truth and declare the emperor naked.

Ultimately, the two deranged characters, one fictitious, the other real, while declaring themselves demi-gods, do not believe in any god at all. They believe in power; power is their god. As the young deranged Pope tells his confessor thus making a mockery of the sacrament of confession: "God, my conscience does not accuse me, because you do not believe I am capable of repenting, and therefore, I do not believe in you. I do not believe you are capable of saving me from myself." When the confessor is shocked by what he just heard, the Pope replies that it was just a joke.

So, what we have are two nine year olds desperately looking for love and understanding while their pathologies place the whole world in peril. This is surrealistic stuff of high quality, a reality show worthy of a Fellini movie, entertaining, fascinating, but also quiete disquieting. An American Pope who does not believe in God, and an American President who does not believe in democracy and the constitution that gave birth to the country of which he is president. But the best of the reality show may still be in the making.

Essay 12

HONOR, ETHICS, SHAME, GUILT AND CIVILIZATION

Figure 12.1. To be or not to be, that is the question.

A shame culture, as the dictionary defines it, involves a society putting "high emphasis on preserving honor" and not being publicly disgraced." People conform to societal norms, independent form the fact that those norms may be just social customs having little to do with ethics, for the mere fear of being shamed or dishonored publicly.

In contrast to that we have a guilt culture which the dictionary defines as "the internalization of a moral code." This conformity to a moral code occurs through the free will of man rather than by the public approval of society.

For example, in Homer's epic poem *The Iliad*, what is most valued is honor. To obtain it and the honor that goes with it one must do glorious deeds (such as fighting as a great warrior would), or, more intellectually, be a great orator, speaking well in the assembly and being highly skilled with words; or being a great philosopher like Socrates or Plato or Aristotle. Thus one acquires goods and rewards that publicly signify and represent the honor conferred: medals, certificates, diplomas, honorary titles, etc., attesting to the merits and the superiority of one individual man over another.

In contrast we can observe that in *The Histories of Herodotus* the social world is less dominated by aspects of shame; more emphasis is placed on guilt. Instead of being publicly shamed into following certain social norms, the individual compels a code of conduct or morality on him/herself, motivated by the guilt she/he feels for not observing society's condoned behaviors. He may even observe such a code even were he living in isolation from any kind of organized governed society, even absent punishments by the police and the justice system for infractions of the law.

This difference can even be easily observed in the depictions of the gods within those two disparate societies: one based on shame and honor, the other based on guilt and duty to oneself and one's human nature. For example, in Homer's *Iliad* the gods are present everywhere anthropomorphically, with all the weaknesses and defects of men, to be sure, albeit their powers and virtues are superior to man, idealized, so to speak. It's the modern Nietzchean "Uberman" or the Freudian "Superego" being actualized mythically and poetically. The gods are almost "beyond good and evil," above moral norms, transcending mere human customs and behavior. Hence the famous Platonic question: are the gods good because they observe the law, or are they good because they are above the law; are they obliged by the law and morality as humans are? But in Herodotus' *Histories*, the gods appear very rarely and, rather than being depicted as humans with extraordinary superpowers, are strangely portrayed in ways that would suggest human behavioral norms.

Figure 12.2. Honor and shame on different paths.

Jumping now to modern times, Giambattista Vico in his *The New Science* (1725) teaches us that a sign of a decaying civilization is the degradation and impoverishment of language, language being a sine qua non of any sort of civilization and indeed an integral part of being human. But there are two other important characteristics which are also part of human nature: the ability to laugh and the ability to feel shame. Here too, when those two characteristics wane, so does civilization.

I'd like to reflect briefly on the latter within the context of our present cultural predicaments. The initial inquiry is this: is shame natural to man or is it something acquired with culture? The answer to that question is crucial since it determines whether or not it is shamelessness that is the acquired trait. To put it another way: could it be that the beauty that we humans are capable of as we live with each other derives from the fact that man is naturally a blushing creature; the only creature in fact capable of blushing?

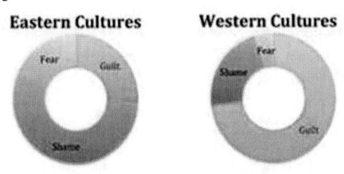

Figure 12.3. Traits of Eastern and Western cultures.

Plato for one, saw a connection between self-restraint and self-government or democracy, and therefore he saw a political danger in promoting the fullest self-expression or indulgence. That may explain his suspicions of artists in general. For Plato, to live together requires rules and a governing and restraint of the passions. Those who live without shame are unruly and unrulable. That is to say, they have lost the ability to restrain themselves by the observation of the rules they collectively have given themselves. One can easily extrapolate from *The Republic* that tyranny is the natural mode of government for the shameless and the self-indulgent; the government of those who have carried liberty beyond any sort of restraint, be it natural or conventional.

What the ancient Greeks were saying basically, was that democracy, more than any other form of government requires self-restraint to be inculcated through moral education and imposed through laws. Those laws include the manner of public amusement. Indeed, it would be enough to think of Rome under such tyrannical emperors as Caligula or Nero. Those emperors allowed the people to freely indulge themselves with bread and circus, for indulgence did not threaten their rule which did not depend on citizens of good character. The formula is here inverted: the more debased the citizenry, the more they are distracted by pleasurable activities, the safer the tyrant's rule and power are.

And here we come to what is obscene and offensive. What are we to make of the obscenity employed by some of the greatest of our poets, the likes of Aristophanes, Dante, Chaucer, Shakespeare and Swift, never mind the Marquis de Sade, just to mention a few. They wrote a good deal of obscenity. How do we account for it? Aristotle in his Poetics hints at a plausible answer: comedy makes us laugh at what is ludicrous in ugliness, and its purpose is to teach, just as tragedy teaches by making us cry before what is destructive in nobility. For Aristotle they are equally serious and Shakespeare would agree, for he was both a comic and a tragic poet. Which is not to imply that both Aristotle and Shakespeare were unable to discern the emperor wearing no clothes, and performing unnatural acts to boot. Nowadays we have an emperor who goes around naked of any moral sensibilities but wants us to believe that he is wearing splendid clothes. A few people, the more courageous among us, have dared to yell "the emperor is naked,"

What artists such as Mapplethorpe have attempted in the brave new world of present Western civilization is to aestheticize the obscene by deliberately choosing subjects that shock the normal sense of decency. Those artists count on and exploit a dual reaction: to create tension in the viewer so that what is indecent and immoral becomes beautiful and therefore especially disturbing. The pretension is that the emperor is not naked, that obscenity is not there; that it resides only in the dirty minds of the viewers who are unable to appreciate beauty. What those artists are doing in effect is to deny the viewers their right to be shocked when they try hard to do exactly that. Is this having the cake and eating it too?

The "enlightened" modern art connoisseur and practitioner will of course retort: but this is art and art is free of any constraints! Indeed, it is but let us be honest with ourselves and admit that indeed great art may be used immorally for the furtherance of an ideology or for propaganda purposes neglectful of the truth (remember the documentary film about Hitler "Triumph of the Will"?), just as a saint may produce banal art, for as Emmanuel Kant has taught us in his *The Critique of Judgment* there is no strict nexus between the moral and the aesthetic and there is no need for morality to slavishly submit to the claims of Art. The public ought to remain free to subsidize or not to subsidize those "enlightened" modern artist without being branded "cultural philistines" by those who think that anything goes in art.

The ancient Greeks were also aware that those aspects of the soul that makes man truly human require political life. Man's virtues and their counterparts, man's vices, require that he be governed and to govern. But the poet knows with Rousseau and the romantics that there is a beauty beyond the polity, the beauty of the natural order. The world of convention is not the only world. Here obscenity may play a part. Obscenity can indeed be used to ridicule the conventional. In the hands of a poet obscenity can serve to elevate above the conventional order in which most of us are forced to live our mundane lives full of quite desperation; lives who never dare ask that dreadful existential question: what is the point of it all, which the Greeks rendered with one word: the Logos. Which is to say, in the hands of a poet, obscenity's purpose becomes that of teaching what is truly beautiful, not what convention holds to be beautiful.

How to express a distinction between the justified and the unjustified use of obscenity in a rule of law is easier said than done. Certainly children are not capable of the distinction, they cannot grasp irony, and need to be protected. One thing is sure though, there are dire consequences resulting from the inability to distinguish between the proper and the improper use of obscenity. When the distinction is forgotten, when we conclude that shame itself is unnatural, that we must get rid of our hang ups and give up the conventions devised by hypocrites, that there are no judgments to be made, that nothing that is appropriate in one place is inappropriate in another place (for just as a dog is not prevented from copulating in the market place, so it is unnatural to deprive men of the same pleasure were it only that of the voyeur in a theater) we will then also have forgotten the distinction between art and trash; that is to say, we will have made ourselves shameless.

Essay 13

A NEW WORLD ORDER: THE END OF PAX AMERICANA AND PUTIN'S ENIGMATIC NEW RUSSIANNESS

Figure 13.1. The end of America's hegemony?

If one surveys Putin's official pronouncements of the last few years on Russia's historical role in the 21st century, one may soon notice that the language of ideological fanaticism, so prevalent during the Soviet era, has slowly evolved in that of values, character, spiritual identity, tradition and historical heritage. At first blush it appears that it's no longer a game of raw power and economics, but one of "soft power," if not exactly that of reasoned philosophical dialogue, morality, and spiritual vision.

The question arises: has the leopard changed its spots? Is this a new ideology based on a vision, on the "inner strength" to be discovered in centuries upon centuries of Russian history and spiritual ties, the way a Dostoevsky understood it? In other words, while acknowledging that Russia is not the West with its particular notions of electoral democracy, freedom of speech, and human rights, Mr. Putin and company would like to promote the idea that Russia remains unique: it is not bourgeois, essentially greedily capitalistic; it is no longer tied to the Communist ideology, nor is it corrupt and decadent as the West.

Figure 13.2. Dostoevsky. The greatest of novelists?

A corollary question arises: is this a new, less ideological, definition of Russianness? A mishmash of patriotism coupled to religious fervor

(Russian Orthodoxy), the cult of the mother, sports, and the resurgence of provincial intelligentsia? Putin, after all, seems to be a genius in finding out what people want and then cleverly manipulating them. There is an affinity here with Donald Trump's kind of populism, which may go a long way in explaining their mutual, if perplexing, admiration and sympathy.

The conundrum persists however, for there is a colossal lack of trust between Putin and his people despite what he claims about his own popularity. If truth be told, it is a trumped up popularity due to the fact that he totally controls and manipulates the media, and just about everything else that transpires in Russia. Restoring that trust may prove harder than articulating a new national idea.

Many Russians no longer accept the idea of being subjects of the State; they wish to be citizens contributing to its overall prosperity. Here Putin and his oligarchs, who have greatly enriched themselves after the demise of the Soviet Union, leave much to be desired. Until that trust is restored and people feel that their aspirations, input and contributions are respected, beginning with credible and legitimate elections, authoritarianism will continue to increase in Russia at the expense of a truly democratic society.

Be that as it may, let's return to the struggle, be it cultural, or be it geopolitical, between Russia and the West. It's hard to imagine a period, since the end of the Cold War, when relations between Russia and the US have been so disastrous. What happened to the new era, the so called reset, which the end of the Cold War was supposed to usher in? Some political science experts today talk of a New Cold War, others mention an enormous misunderstanding in the grasping of a new Russia and the new ideology as above delineated, which of course they alone are able to understand and explain. It gets pretty confusing. Let's see if we can unravel the confusion.

The undeniable fact is that Russia, since the end of the Soviet Empire, has returned to the world stage with a vengeance, wielding an agenda that wants to appear visionary, for Russians at any rate, but looks progressively more and more Machiavellian, aiming at a restoration of power and prestige on the international stage. It seems to be eager to redress the real or perceived slights perpetrated by the West, NATO and the Atlantic alliance, and restore a semblance of its former global role. Some have imputed this attitude to the slightly paranoid narcissistic mind of a former KBG operative named Vladimir Putin.

But the question persists. Where did it all go wrong with the relationship and who is to blame? Is it a question of US overreaching or one of Russia's nostalgia for Soviet imperial greatness buttressed by a brand new powerful ideology? Since the economy of Russia is smaller than that of Italy and California, is it gambling it all on nuclear weapons and intimidation, and perhaps cyber wars and disinformation, not too dissimilar to misguided strategy of the North Koreans? To answer that question may require a book the length of Dostoyevsky's *The Brothers Karamazov*, but a few brief pointers may have to suffice for the moment.

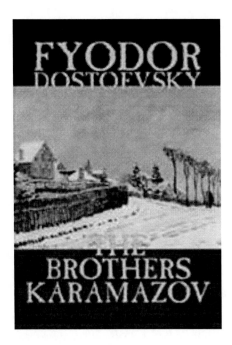

Figure 13.3. Dostoevsky's Brothers Karamozov.

Perhaps the initial fault does lie with the West, after all. It began when the West miserably failed to treat Russia as a nation that had mustered the courage to shake off Soviet Communism. Instead of welcoming it into a new community of nations, NATO treated it almost as a successor state to the USSR, inheriting the distrust of the West toward it.

Russia was later admitted into the G7 club making it the G8, but not as a full respected member but as an observer. This mistake was compounded when the West enthusiastically approved NATO's expansion into Poland, the Czech Republic, Hungary, countries with their own nationalistic traditions of struggle against Moscow's rule. Then it added the Baltic States who also had been satellites of the Soviet Union. Should we really wonder why Russia is so adamant about stopping the absorbing of Georgia and the Ukraine into NATO's orbit and that Putin may be already eyeing those Baltic countries while pursuing a strategy of divide and conquer. That strategy is quite apparent even in the Western part of the EU where ultra-nationalistic movements are being funded and interference in those countries' elections is being practiced via misinformation and cyber-warfare. As the Norwegian TV series makes clear, those occupations are now "silk occupations."

Of course there is another side to this coin, that of the West which prefers to speak of Russian "revanchism" as personified by Vladimir Putin who once described the collapse of the Soviet Union as "the greatest geopolitical catastrophe of the 20th century." Lately he has been showing an extremely assertive behavior in the Ukraine, Georgia, and Syria. And of course the experts continue debating which side is right, while Putin continues his strategy of divide and conquer.

It must be acknowledged however that presently there is no discernible politically super-charged ideological competition going on, one resembling the one that went on in the Cold War. And that is a good thing in itself. There is however a competition for influence and here it must be admitted that economically Russia is still a power of a lesser order. The temptation remains for Russia to try desperate measures by the vaunting of its nuclear weapons or its new found less expensive weapon: weaponized misinformation and cyber-warfare with which to interfere in other countries' internal affairs, and about which the US Congress is presently investigating in regard to the 2016 presidential election.

While it may be true that Pax Americana is over, and a firmer NATO alliance, based on cooperation and trust, is urgently needed, a new reset button with Russia is nowhere on the horizon right now. In any case, for the sake of global peace and stability, should a new warmer sort of relationship with Russia be envisioned?

The experts will of course continue to explain away to demonstrate their expertise. The spies will Machiavellically continue to misinform and conduct cyber warfare, but in the final analysis history will render the final verdict on this thorny conundrum. History may occasionally offer a different interpretation in the light of subsequent events, but it does not deceive and misinform. The wiser course is to rely on the historical judgment on whether or not Putin and Trump represent the future or a blundering repetition of the past.

Essay 14

DEMOCRACY: THE MISSING INGREDIENT IN THE BANNON/DUGIN CONCEPT OF EURASIANISM

Figure 14.1. Two fellow conspiracy theorists and idealogues.

A strange phenomenon is observable lately among experts on Russia-US relations. There is a trend to explain the various thorny intricacies of such a relationship merely via economic strategies and formulas.

The narrative usually begins with the end of World War II when the World Bank (otherwise known as the Marshall Plan) was set up to help in the reconstruction of Europe, something whose success is usually praised by the experts. The main genial idea was that of giving rather than lending money to the tune of 13 billion dollars, in order to restore the economy of 17 EU countries (in today's currency value it would be the equivalent of 120 billion dollars) as long as those countries agreed to use the money to buy goods from the US.

Then the narrative seems to jump some 40 years or so to the dissolution of the Soviet Union and the setting up of the Western economically prosperous camp under NATO's and the EU's influence, and the Eastern camp under the influence of Russia. So, having eliminated ideological beliefs and strife (i.e., Communism vs. Capitalism) the split is now a mere spheres of influence opposition. This, so the argument goes, could have been easily eliminated if Russia had been economically been integrated into the G7 and brought up to speed, but alas it did not happen and that explains the present geo-political turmoil; in other words, if another Marshall Plan had been devised benefitting the whole Eastern region.

At first blush it seems to make sense, but it's a bit too facile and naïve. There are truths here, but there are also half-truths and false assumptions. It assumes that indeed ideology and political principles have simply disappeared in the world; that a sort of "end of history" has occurred. The fact is that they have not, and that is discernible not by what there is but what is missing, namely Democracy, what was also missing during the Soviet era. Let's dig a bit deeper into this analysis.

Indeed it is true that the Marshall Plan, within the World Bank, was set up specifically to help a devastated Western Europe and foment its economic development. In effect the Marshall Plan replaced the World Bank. It was decided that the reconstruction of Europe would be more efficient and cost-effective than mere loans. But the ultimate goal of this economic program was to buttress the capitalistic Western democratic block against the undemocratic Easter bloc sponsored by the USSR. This has to be kept firmly in mind when suggesting that a second Marshall plan should have been created after the fall of the Berlin wall or one risks comparing orange and apples.

It needs to be mentioned also that the US government has learned from the mistakes made in the 1920s and 1930s. At the end of the First World War, the Treaty of Versailles, imposed on Germany the payment of huge compensations for war debt and reparation. Germany soon found it difficult to pay and this led to social discontent. The Wall Street crash that occurred in 1929 brought on a global economic crisis. The US drastically reduced capital outflow. Germany stopped paying its debt to France, Belgium and Britain, and these countries in turn stopped paying their debts to the United States. The more industrialized world sank into recession and massive unemployment, and international trade plummeted. To prepare for a different outcome after WWII, Washington decided on policies that would be completely different from those implemented after WWI and until the early 1930s. It set up the Bretton Woods institutions and the United Nations. This was the international institutions approach.

The US government's major concern at the end of the Second World War was to maintain the full employment that it had achieved thanks to the tremendous war effort. It also wanted to guarantee that there would be a trade surplus in relations between the US and the rest of the world. But the major industrialized countries that could import US commodities were literally penniless. For European countries to be able to buy US goods they had to be provided with lots of dollars. But how? Through grants or through loans? To put it simply, the US reasoned as follows: if we lend to our European allies the money they need to rebuild their economy, how are they going to pay us back? They will no longer have the dollars we lent them since they used them to buy from us. In all, there were three possibilities: first possibility, Europe pays back in kind. If this happens European goods will compete with ours on our home market, full employment will be jeopardized and profits will fall. This is not a good solution.

Second possibility, Europe pays back with dollars. They cannot use the dollars they received on loan to pay us back since they have used them to buy our goods. Consequently, if they are to pay us back, we have to lend them the same amount again, plus interest. The risk of being caught in an infernal cycle of indebtedness (which puts a stop to or slows down the smooth running of business) is added to the risk attached to the first possibility. To reduce their debts towards us the Europeans they will try to sell their goods on our home market. They will thus get some of the dollars they need to pay us back, but this will not be enough to rid them of their debts and it will endanger employment in the US.

We are left with the third possibility: we give Europe the money with which to recover. Rather than lend to Europeans (through the World Bank or otherwise) it seems appropriate to give them the dollars they need to build up their economy within a fairly short time. Europeans will use these dollars to buy goods and services from the US. This will guarantee an outlet for US exports which will help to maintain full employment. Once economic reconstruction is achieved Europeans will not be riddled with debts and will be able to pay for what they buy from the US. The US authorities thus concluded that it would be better to proceed by grants, and therefore launched the Marshall Plan.

To those grants in the framework of the Marshall Plan we must add the partial cancellation of France's debt to the US in 1946 (2 bn USD were written off). Similarly Belgium benefited from a reduction of its debt to the US as compensation for the uranium provided to make the first two atomic bombs which were dropped on the Japanese cities of Hiroshima and Nagasaki causing the first nuclear holocaust. The uranium had been extracted from the mine of Shinkolobwé (near Likasi, then Jadotville) located in the province of Katanga in the Belgian Congo. In the first instance: Belgium was granted debt cancellation thanks to the natural resources from its colony, which it lavishly exploited. Then: some fifteen years later, Belgium transferred, to the newly independent Congo, the debts it had incurred in order to exploit those natural resources as well as its population.

From the end of the Second World War until today major powers have refused to implement a Marshall plan for developing countries (with two exceptions, South Korea and Taiwan). Loans with interest have been the main instrument used to allegedly finance the Third World's development. Such refusal shows that creditors do not really want these countries to develop and be rid of their debts. Creditors consider that it is in their better interest to maintain developing countries in a permanent state of indebtedness so as to draw maximum revenues in the form of debt reimbursement, but also to enforce policies that serve their interests and to make sure that they remain loyal partners within the international institutions.

What the United States had done through the Marshall Plan for industrialized countries that had been ravaged by war they exceptionally repeated towards South Korea and Taiwan, two allied developing countries at strategic locations on the outskirts of the Soviet Union and China. As from the 1950s these two countries received significant aid that largely contributed to their economic success.

It all goes to show that there is a nexus between democracy and social distributive justice. The greater the gap between the rich and the poor, the weaker democracy seems to get.

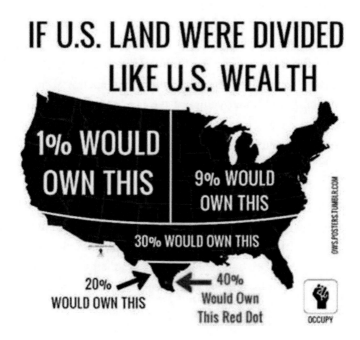

Figure 14.2. Nexus between distributive justice and democracy.

Economists and geo-political area experts are now asking the crucial question: why was not a new Marshall Plan devised for the impoverished Eastern countries (former satellites of the Soviet Empire) after the fall of the Berlin Wall? It would have indeed made eminent sense if we stay with economic considerations. But there is another important consideration and it is the consideration of Democracy and a new ideology called Eurasianism to which we turn next.

What is Eurasianism? It is a kind of prophetic vision envisioning Russia's destiny as that of leading all Slavic and Turkic people in a grand empire to resist corrupt Western values. Its main proponent is Alexander Dugin. His philosophy glorifies the Russian Empire—while on the Western side of the equation Bannon and the conservative website that he founded, Breitbart News, has revived the slogan of "America first."

What Bannon and Dugin have in common is the idea that global elites have conspired against ordinary people—and the old order must be overthrown. In the West this is called populism. As Dugin declared to Newsweek: "We have arrived at a moment where the world is discovering a new model of ideologies. The election of Trump shows that clearly."

Eurasianism seems like a mutual admiration society: Bannon admires Dugin for placing traditional values at the heart of the nationalistic revival and he has said as much at a Vatican Conference he attended in 2014. Dugin admires Bannon for rejecting Western liberalism.

One may ask: which are their common enemies? They are secularism, multiculturalism, egalitarianism and what both Dugin and Bannon dub the "globalized and internationalist capitalist liberal elite." Which is to say, the global ideological struggles will be reduced to an ultimate struggle between culturally homogenous—mostly white-homogenous groups founded on Judeo-Christian values and practicing a humane sort of capitalism, and the international crony-capitalist network of bankers and businessmen.

Both Bannon and Dugin wish to revive the nation-state. Hence their support for anti-European Union candidates from England and France to Hungary and Greece. They both are firmly against pan-European Union. In the US they have invented the Deep State or what they see an over-centralized government but paradoxically they'd rather have a strong state with an authoritarian personality on top, one that in effect ignores the freedoms as set-up by the founding fathers to be controlled at the local level.

In order to appear democratic and not ethnic chauvinists both Dugin and Bannon have declared that they believe in multi-civilizations which have their own identity and destiny and follow their own course. They have both described themselves as revolutionaries; Bannon has described himself as a Leninist who wants to destroy the State (i.e., the Deep State), while Dugin is the founder of the National Bolshevik Party which has been fomenting armed uprising among Russian minorities in former Soviet Republics. In any case, those states are always white and non-Asian, which of course is redolent of the theory of the "super-race" of Hitler and Mussolini.

So it comes as no great surprise that Trump's election was greeted with enthusiasm in Russia. Trump would give Russia the respect it has so far been denied. St. Petersburg's Cossacks have given Trump the honorary title of "captain" in case he decides with Bannon, to "make Russia great again."

But this love-fest has been rather short-lived. Bannon has not continued to advocate the lifting of sanctions on Russia (imposed after Crimea's annexation in 2014), nor the lifting of a travel ban on Dugin (imposed when he acclaimed Putin for taking over Crimea and invading the Ukraine) as he had previously hinted at. After all there are allegations making the round of contacts between Trump advisers in the White House and Russian spies. Suddenly Trump has become "tough on Russia." At this point the appearance of collusion needs to be avoided at any cost, so as not to encourage the FBI to dig any deeper.

Lastly let's see what the reaction to these economic explanation has been among the nations of the EU. What is missing in those experts' analysis is the concept of Democracy. Let's begin with England that has already divorced the EU. Theresa May is treating Britain to a surprise election in June. Even politicians have been blind-sided.

Were one to ask "what do so many disparate nations of the EU have in common?" one could find plenty of cultural common strains, but in purely political terms, perhaps the most apt answer may be "democracy." That is the concept that seems obvious but one hardly ever hears in the debates and discussions about the possible dissolution of the EU, even when referenda and elections are taking place.

Figure 14.3. Inbalance in distributive justice.

There is much bickering over fish, farms, cheese, sausages, pork pies, you name it, but little concern with what unites and what divides 27 disparate countries that consider themselves a super-confederated nation with common values and goals. One hears about differences over currency, the return of sovereign rights control of one's borders, which are paramount concerns of a rabid ultra-nationalism as practiced by a La Farge, or a Wilder or a Le Pen, or a Bossi.

But one hears little about Free Speech or the ability to argue every detail of an issue without fear of arrest or worse. Never mind that democracy remains the only indispensable pre-requisite needed to join the EU.

What one hears is increasing advocacy for exit from the EU. One such example dubbed Brexit is already in place. The election of April 23 may determine if France and others will follow. Authoritarianism is on the rise and the putrid smell of dictatorship is in the air, Recep Tayyip Erdogan took control of his country out of the hands of the people, in effect turning his back on the model of democracy enjoyed in Europe, meanwhile he continues arguing for access to the EU and its single market. That's now unlikely to happen.

What's happening in the Ukraine is just as bad. There Russian President Vladimir Putin takes Ukraine's desire to tip toward democracy as an insult. He is quite good in his rhetoric describing an overreaching NATO encroaching on regions of historic Russian interest, but what the experts out to defend him forget is that the vast majority of Ukrainians despise his manipulations of the media and the economy.

Meanwhile at the EU's borders the anti-democratic forces are converging. They smell blood in the water. Erdogan for one, not unlike Donald Trump, treats every EU negotiation as business deal of sorts. Take the refugee deal: it started off as 3 billion euros in aid which quickly became 6 billion euros. Not to speak of America where we have a president, so called, that treats the nation as a corporation to be fleeced and all political issues as business deals. Democracy is indeed in mortal peril.

Figure 14.4. Oligarchy as part of the economic system.

Then there is Putin whose strategy seems to be that of "divide and conquer, not so much by brute military or economic force, where he knows he will be beaten, but by breaking up the EU's unity and its resolve to punish his land grabs and flagrant violations of international law. Neither men give a damn for North Atlantic values, never mind that of democracy itself. Their appetite for power creates a powerful contrast with what the EU has in common: Democracy and the democratic process which allows the likes of Theresa May to hold snap elections and be assured that the outcome will be free and fair. The same cannot be said for Russia or Turkey.

Nobody will be voting to end democracy, which in fact is not on the ballot in any EU country, but that may not be sufficient to stop democracy from being placed on the backburner while good old xenophobic nationalism gets moved to the front. Ultimately, if democracy is not worth fighting over, nothing is. That, I dare say, is the challenge that the Russia experts have yet to deal with.

Essay 15

THE STUBBORN FACTS ON EUROCENTRISM: NOSTALGIA FOR THE COLD WAR, MISINFORMATION, AND THE RUSSIAN NATIONAL IDENTITY DISCOURSE

Figure 15.1. A new Cold War?

> *"Who would want to associate oneself with the zone of today's Europe, where traditional values are destroyed, homosexualism is on the rampage, there is a migration crisis etc. Europe today is, in essence, a dying zone, where the population is unable to defend its cultural and religious identity. It is a post-Christian and post-European world, a graveyard of European civilization."*
>
> -*Andrei Fursov*, Nationalist Russian Historian

There is an intriguing phenomenon going on in academic and diplomatic-political circles as we speak, especially those circles who deal with the Russia-EU relationship, détente, the Cold War, the present impasse among the two blocks.

On one hand there are those experts who seem almost nostalgic for the Cold War when things were much simpler and complicated matters could be sorted out ideologically: democracy vs. tyranny, as one side saw it, or social justice vs. exploitative capitalism, as the other saw it. Those experts see Russian aggression everywhere, especially in the EU, spearheaded by the events in the Ukraine and Crimea, which was snatched away from the Ukraine. They say NATO has been derelict in responding appropriately.

One of those is Kasparov who has been highly critical of Putin for several years. He led the pro-democracy resistance to Putin's regime in Moscow but fled to New York because he feared for his safety. He has been calling on Western democracies, such as the UK, the US, Germany and France, to stop negotiating with Putin because doing so only appears to validate his claim to power back home. In his book *Winter Is Coming: Why Vladimir Putin and the Enemies of the Free World Must Be Stopped*, Kasparov argues that leaders of the free world have appeased rather than confronted Putin since he ascended to the presidency in 1999—allowing the Russian strongman to become a serious threat to liberty throughout the world.

On the other hand, there are those experts who claim that the West after the fall of the USSR and Berlin Wall and the end of the Cold War missed an opportunity by not inviting Russia to join the table of the European NATO nations, in order to contribute to the prosperity and peace the EU had already enjoyed for half a century or so.

Those experts go around lecturing the non-experts, those who don't understand the intricacies of such a relationship, that they have gotten it wrong on Russia and point to the present situation. The position is enigmatic since more often than not those critics will not reveal if their position is based on a neutral analysis or a hidden ideology hiding in plain sight. They prefer to make people wonder, all in the name of a more effective diplomacy. They say: "trust us; we are the experts and know best how to solve the riddle." They call this posture "having an alias" but perhaps it might be better characterized as having the cake and eating it too.

Be that as it may, while refraining here from returning to the probe into the Trump-Russia campaign, we shall take a hard look at Eurocentrism in the Ukraine and how it has impacted the strained relationship. To do so, as objectively and impartially as is humanly possible we shall first look at the stubborn historical facts based on documented events and scientific data, not on opinion, or propaganda, or disinformation, or hidden alias (often parading as privileged expert information to which only experts and diplomats have access), or alternate facts; just the stubborn incontrovertible, ineluctable facts.

Let's enumerate those facts: Russia has broken every arms control treaty pertaining to Europe. Russia's recent snap exercises violate the Vienna Document. Russia has also broken the INF treaty and the EU has known about it since 2008 and has done nothing. Russia has "suspended" its participation in the Treaty on Conventional Armed Forces in Europe, an action that has no legal standing, and has allowed it to break the limits on forces in Europe. It has also broken numerous treaties by invading Ukraine. Moscow also seems prepared to use its nuclear weapons, probably its tactical nuclear missiles, in a first-strike mode either against military targets or against European capitals.

By 2018, Russia will have reached the numerical limits of the new START treaty and will have to draw down to 1,500 strategic weapons as stipulated by the treaty. Based on current figures, this means Russia has to dismantle over 200 weapons within a year. To judge from previous Russian policy, this is not likely to happen. Russia's priority defense project is modernizing its nuclear forces. A look at Russian nuclear and hypersonic weapons programs indicates that Moscow is also building weapons with which to threaten the United States and Europe.

The EU has so far failed to confront those hard facts. It has failed to recognize the hard reality that Europe may no longer be a theater of peace and that even nuclear war is now possible. It relies on the chimera of the "the end of history and ideology" within a global market. The EU may have to consider augmenting its conventional capabilities to prevent Moscow from thinking that it could with impunity pull off another fait accompli like Crimea, and confront NATO with nuclear threats. Real penalties for breaking arms control treaties must be considered. The present ones imposed after the annexation of Crimea are either ineffective or toothless.

Last, but not least, this fact needs to be acknowledged and confronted on both sides: every European government is presently under information attack by Russia which believes that, at least in that field, it is at war with the West. On January 18, 2005, Russian Defense Minister Sergei Ivanov told the Academy of Military Sciences, the official institutional locus of systematic thinking about contemporary war, that "there is a war against Russia under way, and it has been going on for quite a few years. No one declared war on us. There is not one country that would be in a state of war with Russia. But there are people and organizations in various countries who take part in hostilities against the Russian Federation. Indeed, Russia has long believed that it is at war with the West. That essential fact should not be ignored.

After all, the ongoing revelations of the extent of Russian information warfare, subversion, coups and interference in the US and European elections are acts of war and are regarded by Russian writers on contemporary and information warfare as such. But they are also backed up by potent military threats that are used to intimidate Western audiences before a shot is fired.

It ought not be ignored that the EU has allowed this situation to develop by ignoring countless arms control violations, and these agreements constituted the foundation of European security after 1991.

Any discussion and debate on this issue ought not neglect those stubborn facts.

In any case, what the two above described analysis fail to point out is that Putin and his oligarchs are putting forward an alternate form of Russian identity and ultra-nationalism which hasn't been seen since the advent of the ideological Russian revolution a century ago but it has now a new twist: it is accompanied by a Eurocentric comparison which insists that Russia is not only different but better than Europe. In fact, within the wider context of the Russian political debate, the above described analysis would make no sense unless the Western mirror is utilized. All the reader needs to do to be convinced is take an attentive look at the above quote by Andrei Fursov.

It was the broad anti-Western consensus that made the annexation of Crimea and the support for the Donbas separatists possible and in some sense inevitable. Russian leadership has never stopped worrying about subversive Western influences. Against the backdrop of the urban protest movement of 2011–2012, the Euromaidan came to be interpreted as anything but Ukraine's domestic matter: it was seen as instigated by the West and as a repetition of a future 'colour revolution' in Moscow.

This view, shared by the elites and by the pro-Putin masses alike, provided both the motivation and the legitimation for the dramatic foreign policy steps that followed. The Russian society sees itself as a victim of the West, which is aggressively promoting its own norms, institutions and values throughout post-Soviet space. The EU's Eastern Partnership initiative, NATO enlargement, US plans to create anti-ballistic missile defense, the supranational jurisdiction of the European Court for Human Rights, efforts at democracy promotion, support for LGBT rights movement and human rights in general, are all seen as manifestations of Western expansionism.

To defend its sovereignty, culture and independent moral standing, Russia needs to protect its sovereignty in all possible ways, but in particular by emphasizing its unique values, strengthening 'spiritual bonds' within society and beefing up information security – a broad concept that includes control over media, social networks and private communications.

If necessary, it also has to fight back to stave off the prospect of Ukraine's NATO membership and to make sure there are no NATO military bases in Crimea. It made sure of that in 2014 with the annexation of Crimea.

As a result, positive identification with Europe, which was dominant in Russia in the 1990s, was replaced by a sudden reversal and distancing. While in late 1990s around two thirds of Russians believed their country must strive to become an EU member, this share dropped below 25 per cent after Putin's re-election in 2012. Fifty-nine percent of Russians do not consider Russia a European country while only 17 per cent believe that Russia must develop in the same way as Europe. These are stubborn facts and sobering statistics.

From those statistics it can be safely be deduced that the Russian public shares the slogan 'Russia is not Europe', proclaimed by the Ministry of Culture in April 2014.

Nevertheless, it must also be acknowledged that Russian society would still prefer to see relations with both the West and Ukraine improve. Some aspects of the European way of life, such as economic prosperity and rule of law, still remain hugely attractive to the majority of Russians.

Moreover, even as the modality of the identification with Europe changes, Russian national identity discourse remains Eurocentric. While the overall success of the officially declared 'pivot to Asia' remains subject to a heated debate, identity-wise it has definitely not made Russia an Asian country.

Speaking in more general terms, the only way to insist on the uniqueness of Russian traditional values and spirituality is by contrast with what is perceived as Western or European values. That was the way Dostoevsky proceeded. Europe remains the primary Other, which is seen as a geographical space where history unfolds and as a model of social development and well-being. The Ukrainian conflict is viewed against this broad background, as resulting from the irresponsible expansionism of the West. Under this perspective even the annexation of Crimea is interpreted as an act of defense of one's interests. The aggressors are the US, the EU and NATO. And if that is not rampant political paranoia, it's hard to think of what else might be.

But there are problems with this consensus of blaming any conflict on the West's aggression arrived at via a massive state propaganda. There is an economic crisis, corruption in the top leadership or oligarchy, significant inflation, blatant inequality.

The Kremlin astutely mitigates these negatives with xenophobic attitudes deliberately promoted as needed, but the vast majority of Russians would rather have good relations with their neighbors, the Ukraine, the EU and the US. What the Kremlin has indoctrinated into Russians is the belief that they should be unhappy as to how Russia is treated by those neighbors and rivals on the world stage. That is to say, Russia should be thought of and portrayed as the innocent victim or scapegoat.

In conclusion, those crucial questions arise: are we dealing with ethnic nationalism, Soviet imperialist nostalgia, religious cultural revival, civic patriotic fervor? And are all of these compatible with the current broad range of policies observable in Russia but never fully explained by the experts? Is that inability to explain the policies due to sheer confusion and is the confusion deliberate? Or, are those policies buttressed by the fear of Western expansionism and the concern about the subversive effects of Westernization for the spiritual integrity of Russia as a nation?

Whatever the answer is to those questions, it may be wise for the experts to consider that the discourse on an alternative Russian national identity is and remains Eurocentric, that is to say, the task remains that of explaining how Russia may be different from Europe. Perhaps Dostoevsky may be considered a better guide in that respect than the likes of Putin and Fursov.

Essay 16

THE NIGHTMARE OF MODERN DEMOCRACY IN THE AGE OF ALTERNATE FACTS: A SICKNESS UNTO DEATH?

Figure 16.1. Is Democracy committing suicide?

It is common knowledge that democracy was born in ancient Greece some three thousand years ago. What is less well known is that, since then it has had a rocky and unpredictable history. It has always been mistrusted. Globally, it found itself in favor once again in the late 18th century when it was finally understood that democracy is not a privilege granted by the state but something the people earned and protected every day.

Its modern rise, since the birth of the United States of America was slow and even contradictory. Indeed, how can democracy co-exist with slavery and the concept of unalienable rights? It took a bloody civil war to settle that kind of conundrum.

Its rise after that was not instantaneous, but somehow it ended up the default mode of modern politics, first in the whole of Western civilization, particularly its North Atlantic section. By the end of the 20th century, it was spreading rapidly around the world and the prediction of many historians and political scientists was that it would eventually win out over authoritarianism and tyranny.

Alas, that prediction has never come to full fruition. For a few years now, things have not been going so well. The idea of a "transition to democracy" suddenly started to seem like more of a hopeful phrase than an accurate prognosis for countries in the Maghreb and the Middle East. Since the onset of the financial crisis in the west, the debate has been heating up in democratic countries.

The questions arise: is democracy itself in crisis, and if so, why? And what can we do to fix the problem? Anxiety accompanies these questions. We refuse to envision a world without liberty and democracy, but to lie on our laurels and do nothing is to ensure that it comes about.

Let us remember that fascist theoretician Giovanni Gentile dared to write that fascism was "the most genuine form of democracy"; and while inveighing against parliamentary democracy, Nazis denied that the Third Reich was a dictatorship and developed their own conception of "Germanic democracy" into the bargain. Those claims remind us of the thorny problem of the definition of democracy which begins with Plato and ends up with Alexis de Tocqueville, the author of the classic study of democracy in America.

Part of de Tocqueville's appeal rests on his own ambivalence about democracy. Some of the US founding fathers, such as Adams, were also touched by the ambiguity. For him, this new political creed was a force whose advent was unstoppable. He is enthusiastic at some points about democracy's energy and ambition; much less so at what he regarded as its philistinism (the rough cowboy redneck feature) and its drive to a kind of levelling cultural despotism. Writing at a time when it was still possible for a liberal to confess openly to serious doubts about democracy as a system and to conceive of other choices, he is able to surprise modern readers for whom this kind of detachment is no longer even thinkable.

Another striking feature of his acute analysis of Democracy is the emphasis on America. He is the first to remind us that that democracies tend to complacency; and secondly, that in the face of crisis, they manage to muddle through. Except when they don't, the cynic will argue, thinking perhaps of democratic Weimar Germany, but let's also remember that Germany, in practice, never had a politically settled democratic culture.

As mentioned, traditional democracies tend to self-correct. They learn from their mistakes and move on, they adapt, even in the face war and economic crisis. Perhaps a key fact about democracies is that it is never as bad as the doom-and-gloomsters would like to portray it. Does that mean that democracies are more successful in adapting to crisis than other polities? After all did not some successful imperial dynasties last for centuries and even millennia? One thinks of the Ottoman and Habsburg dynasties. American democracy is barely two centuries old. Fascism proved to be pretty adaptable. Mussolini's regime was not brought down from lack of flexibility but by military defeat. Soviet Communism proved quite malleable in the 1920s and the 1930s with its New Economic Policy and the return to private property, then veering toward collectivization. Adaptability seems to be ingrained in most polities; it seems to be part of human nature.

So, what makes democracies unique? Why did democracy prevail over fascism in World War II? Could it be that democracies have a sense of international responsibility to pump the lifeblood of liberty around the world? Isn't that what it means to be world power as a democracy in the 20th and 21st century? Did not the panic that ensued in 1940, when it looked as if Germany might conquer England, leaving the US alone, engender a transatlantic commitment still alive today, albeit presently in peril?

After the dust settled in 1945, few things were more important than rebuilding democracy around the world and showing it could be made compatible with capitalism. Whether such a feat of compatibility is even possible is not our concern here. What concerns me is the fact that the old misgivings about democracy seem to have returned with a vengeance, especially since the election of Donald Trump who has recently refused to acknowledge article five of the NATO treaty. "We can isolate ourselves and go it alone" seems the most recent political slogan, on both sides of the Atlantic. Which is to say that the appetite for democracy-making and remaining a beacon for a world aspiring to liberty and prosperity is also on the wane.

There is currently a dangerous cliffhanger in Washington. Even in Europe there is talk of "going it alone" and withdraw from the Atlantic Alliance. Will muddling through work this time around? This is equivalent to asking the question: how, in a democracy, can those at the helm govern effectively? Is democratic government a contradiction in terms? Is it one thing to have a vision, and another to have a policy and to make it work? Exactly on what is political authority and public action based upon, if not on the consent and a shared sense of purpose with those who are governed? With these questions we are led back to Plato's *Republic*.

To return to the self-correcting, self-perfecting characteristic of democracy, mistakes are there to be embraced rather than denied. Take the financial crisis, for example. Could it be that the crux of the deficit in democracy lies in the postwar social compact punctuated by central bank independence to drive out inflation, financial deregulations and their hangover from the past such as heavy welfare commitment that cannot be funded except through borrowing, and the fiscal implication of an ageing population?

With early 21st-century growth rates weakening, all the conditions are in place for a new repudiation of democracy. The political democratic entity most in danger is the EU, not the US, as most people believe. Greece, the very cradle of democracy, is perhaps the best example. There the fiscal crisis has made a mockery of the national democratic process. It's about to happen in Italy too.

It is hard, as we speak, to be very sanguine about democracy's future within the Transatlantic Alliance. It appears that democracies are nowadays learning less well from their mistakes than they used to in the past. For instance, in the past there were ideological rivals doing things as well, if not better, than many democracies, especially in social welfare, which forced democracies to change their social methods and rethink their nexus to capitalism. That seems to be lacking now.

But there is a second crucial concern and it is the collapse of organized labor which has led to a premature boardroom rejoicing while depriving democracies of a collective capacity to think about long-term effects of private-sector decision making. From there to the denial of climate change and science itself is a short step.

Which is to say, it is not that democracy will die any time soon, but it's that the kind of democracy that now surrounds us with its billionaires (a tiny fraction of the population) controlling most of a nation's wealth, and its unemployed millions, its surveillance state (dubbed Deep State by those who have conspiratorial tendencies), its unelected technocrats, its incompetent bureaucrats and politicians, its individual gratification, and its ever-narrowing vision of the common good. Previous generations would have been alarmed and would have regarded this situation as a nightmare. This is the nightmare about which both Plato and Tocqueville warned us about, the kind of nightmare from which democracy may never awake. In more philosophical Kierkegaardian terms: it is "the sickness unto death": the ones who have it do not know they have it.

Essay 17

POPE FRANCIS'S CRITIQUE OF BANNON'S VIEWS ON CHRISTIANITY

Figure 17.1. Religion and politics.

"Pope Francis wants to break the organic link between culture, politics, institution and Church. Spirituality cannot tie itself to governments or military pacts for it is at the service of all men and women. Religions cannot consider some people as sworn enemies nor others as eternal friends. Religion should not become the guarantor of the dominant classes"

--Rev. Antonio Spadaro and Marcelo Figueroa (in Civiltà Cattolica)

The Rome-based Jesuit publication *La Civiltà Cattolica* is widely considered one of the most influential Vatican journals within Catholic intellectual circles. Recently it has issued a scathing rebuke of certain strands of religious evangelical "fundamentalism" which in its view has fused with politics in America and elsewhere.

The authors are two of the present Pope's confidants: Rev. Antonio Spadaro, and Rev. Marcelo Figueroa. The first is a Jesuit, as the Pope is also, who serves as editor-in-chief of the journal, and the other is a Presbyterian pastor and editor-in-chief of the Argentinian version of the Vatican newspaper "*L'Osservatore Romano.*"

Spadaro has maintained close communication with the pope since Francis' election. Under his watch, *La Civiltà Cattolica* has become one of the foremost vehicles for understanding the views of the current pontificate. While the publication isn't an official Vatican source, it is reviewed by the Vatican's Secretary of State before it is published.

The article explicitly mentions President Donald Trump, who in the past has identified as a Presbyterian, and his adviser Steve Bannon, who identifies as a faithful Catholic, allegedly loyal to Church doctrine.

Figure 17.2. The scholarly Journal of the Vatican.

The article attacks the decades-old partnership between two strands of American Christianity — fundamentalist evangelicals and Catholics who are brought together by the "same desire for religious influence in the political sphere." Although these two groups differ on a number of theological issues, they have come together since the 1980s and 1990s over issues like abortion and same-sex marriage.

Spadaro and Figueroa have accused this group of misinterpreting verses in the Bible to fit their own political stances on a wide range of topics — from war-mongering to climate change to the idea of America as a "promised land" that is to be defended against all odds. This is in conformity with Steve Bannon's professed theory of the invasion of Christian Europe by hordes of Moslem refugees; a theory he gathered from a book titled *The Field of the Saints*.

In this article, the authors explain that these evangelicals and Catholics "condemn traditional ecumenism and yet promote an ecumenism of conflict that unites them in the nostalgic dream of a theocratic type of state." One of the most worrisome aspects of this alliance for the pair is how it encourages hatred of different ethnicities and conflates Islam with terrorism. At a purely political level, this hatred of Moslems has been exemplified in the travel ban President Trump has attempted to put into effect at the outset of his tenure in the White House. The courts, as equal branch of the government, have fortunately intervened in the matter.

In any case, this view of the world stands in stark contrast to Pope Francis' interfaith outreach and his repeated calls to build bridges, not walls. The two authors state that "The most dangerous prospect for this strange ecumenism is attributable to its xenophobic and Islamophobic vision that wants walls and purifying deportations."

They compare Steve Bannon's world view to that of the so-called Islamic State, branding Bannon a "supporter of an apocalyptic geopolitics." They claim this vision of the world reduces everything to a battle between good and evil, between God and Satan, and that moreover "the desire of these Christian fundamentalists is to submit the state to the Bible with a logic that is no different from the one that inspires Islamic fundamentalism. We must not forget that the theo-politics spread by Isis is based on the same cult of an apocalypse that needs to be brought about as soon as possible."

Then the authors outline the path that Pope Francis recommends in stark contrast to this "apocalyptic" view of politics and religion. They claim that the pope "radically rejects" the idea of creating an actual Kingdom of God here on earth through politics, including at the level of a political party...Spirituality cannot tie itself to governments or military pacts for it is at the service of all men and women. Religions cannot consider some people as sworn enemies nor others as eternal friends. Religion should not become the guarantor of the dominant classes."

Those are strong admonishing words that should put to rest once and for all the misguided notion that the likes of Steve Bannon and Paul Ryan are good Catholics who espouse the magisterial teaching of the Catholic Church. They are far from being good Catholics, and a sure sign that such may be the case is their enthusiastic identification with social Darwinistic, racial, and class theories of White Supremacy supporting the privileged and the rich and condemning the poor and the underprivileged of our world.

Essay 18

DARKNESS AT TWILIGHT: THE DEVIL'S BARGAIN IN AMERICAN POLITICS?

Figure 18.1. Will the light overcome the darkness?

"America is a shining city on the hill"

--President Ronald Reagan

"Darkness is good...Don't let up"

--Steve Bannon to Donald Trump

To get a clearer idea of how far down the hill American politics have tumbled, all we need to do is to pause and reflect on the two quotes above, and then peruse the recently released book by journalist Joshua Green on Steve Bannon and the rise of Trump to the US presidency. The book's title is *Devil's Bargain: Steve Bannon, Donald Trump and the Storming of the Presidency.*

Like the book we are about to survey, the two quotes convey the enormous political ideological journey downward the Republican party has traveled within 30 short years. It couldn't be more clear: we have traveled backward, from light, or at least a desire for the light, to darkness celebrated as something good and desirable. Are there echoes here of *Darkness at Noon* by British novelist Arthur Koestler (1940)?

Those are interesting speculations, but the crucial question is: How have we managed to reach such a sad state of affairs? Here the book in question could provide useful suggestions. In the first place the book debunks the myth that Bannon, whom some have called the shadow president of America, is the Rasputin of the White House spinning Apocalyptic conspiracies and directing the chaotic traffic of Trump's White House West Wing. He may be that, but he is much more menacing. While he may be at the center of the palace intrigues at the WH, he is also a discerning barometer by which we can determine who is in favor and who is out of favor. The pendulum seems to swing between the nationalists and the globalists.

Naturally Bannon champions the nationalists when it comes to immigration or trade, but his overall theory dictates the dismantling of the American checks and balances system and the embracing of a crude populism which appears as anti-elitism and anti-privilege but is in reality a cover to consolidate the power and influence of the 10% privileged citizens of the Republic. At least that's the case for Trump who has no ideas and incapable of an ideology. The two men are in fact using each other. Bannon's is the mind-set of the consummate fanatical ideologue intersecting at the right moment with that of the charlatan opportunistic deal-maker presenting itself as an empty suit hungry for power and wealth.

In that respect Bannon, as a brilliant ideologue crashing on the American political scene from its fringes, may have already done enough ruinous damage to the GOP and the country in general, which may go on even without Trump as standard bearer. The ultimate aim, even independent of Trump, seems to be that of reshaping the Republican party, a strategy that Bannon had envisioned even before he joined the Trump entourage. Even more than reshaping it, it aims at its utter destruction.

How will this demolition project work? Here again Green's book provides some hints. It suggests that we ought to begin the analysis in 2012 when Bannon took over the far-right news site Breitbart. Immediately one notices the nativist populism of Bannon's views. There was also an apparent enthusiasm to attack all globalist Republicans. One of the targets was Paul Ryan portrayed as a secret admirer of the Clintons.

This situation escalated rapidly once Bannon was on board the Trump campaign in the summer of 2016. It went far beyond the expulsion of ideological enemies from the Republican party. In the fall of 2016 Trump begins to channel Bannon conspiratorial world view tying it to Hillary Clinton's global power structure responsible for the robbing of the working class in America, stripped it of its wealth and put the money in the pockets of large corporations. Of course Trump presented himself not as integral part of such power structure but as the champion of the poor and disadvantaged. Populism and nativism worked to perfection on people whose wages had stagnated since the Reagan years in the 80s. Trump would lead them from victory to victory, to the point that they would "get tired of winning." Spoken as a genuine used-car salesman. Jews smelled anti-Semitism immediately in this Bannonian ideology and protested it vehemently, to which Bannon reportedly retorted that "darkness is good," and then advised Trump: "don't let up."

Examining the first six months of Trump's presidency, one must sadly conclude that the darkness far from letting up, has progressed incrementally. The GOP and American democracy in general are now in the process of accommodating themselves to it, while Bannon boasts that he has provided a platform for the alt-right. That in effect translates in sexual bias, racism, xenophobia, and nativism.

Bannon's darkness seems to be enveloping more and more of the proverbial shining city on the hill. Previous fringe ideas, especially conspiracy theories on the Democratic party ("The Deep State" theory is one of them), or on refugees, or on globalists, are now gaining mainstream status and deemed respectable. Scapegoating, incivility and disrespect for truth and honesty are rampant. That may do more damage and lasting impact to American pluralistic democracy than Trump's deranged personality itself.

The book overall conveys a sense of reductive determinism redolent of the historical theories of Bannon at the expense of human freedom which may still be able to reverse the situation. That may well be the greatest weakness of the book. Without human freedom hope becomes problematic. While keeping our eyes open to the reality of the darkness following the crepuscular twilight of sunset, we need to remember that the light of dawn breaks out when the darkness of the night is at its most profound. But the question persists: do we still dare hope?

ABOUT THE AUTHOR

Emanuel L. Paparella
Barry University,
Miami Shores, FL, USA
emanuelpaparella@yahoo.com

INDEX

A

Abelard, 17
Acton, Lord, 77
Adams, John, 155
Adorno, 61
Avyagintsev, Andrei, 94

B

Bacon, Francis, 118, 119
Bannon, Steven, 109, 115, 160, 161, 162, 164
Barth, Karl, 19
basil, 15, 16, 95
Benjamin, 61
Berlusconi, 118
Bernard, 17
Bertrand del Bornio, 73
Blondel, Maurice, 54
Bretton Woods, 137
Brexit, 94, 120, 143
Buchanan, Pat, 93, 97

C

Caligula, viii, 101, 110, 117, 118, 120, 126
Calvin, John, 18
Campbell, Joseph, vii, 23, 24
Casanova, Josè, 81
Centesimus Annus, 90
Charlemagne, 16, 58, 79
Chesterton, G.K., 80
Civiltà Cattolica, 160
Clinton, Hillary, 165
Cohen, Hermann, 73
Colet, John, 21

D

Dante, vii, x, 17, 27, 28, 49, 50, 64, 65, 66, 67, 73, 79, 118, 127
Dawson, Christopher, 14, 20, 50, 52, 75
 The Making of Europe, 20, 52, 75, 76, 78
Day, Dorothy, 14
democracy, v, vi, viii, ix, x, 1, 2, 4, 5, 28, 57, 67, 83, 88, 90, 101, 102, 115, 121, 122, 126, 130, 135, 136, 139, 140, 141,

142, 143, 144, 146, 149, 153, 154, 155, 156, 157, 165, 166
liberal, vii, ix, x, 1, 4, 5, 8, 11, 17, 18, 19, 41, 42, 43, 46, 47, 87, 140, 155
Demosthenes, 16
Derridà, Jacques, 70
Descartes, 52, 55, 56, 67, 72
Dostoevsky, Fyodor, 130, 150, 151
Dugin, Alexander, 140

E

Einstein, Albert, 56, 78
Eisenstadt, Shmuel, 50, 83
Eliot, T.S., 67
Epicurus, 52
Erasmus, Desiderius, 14
Erdogan, Recep Tayyip, 143
Eurasianism, viii, 135, 140
European Union, 41, 51, 57, 60, 61, 67, 86, 90, 91, 140
    EU Constitution, 43, 86
    European Integration, 85, 87, 89, 90
    Goddess Europa, 71
    Spiritual Idea of Europe, 54

F

Feuerbach, 59
Ficino, Marsilio, 15
Fortuyn, Pim, 47
Fra Angelico, 79, 80
Frank, Thomas, 104
Fry, Christopher, 14
Fursov, Andrei, 146, 149
    Winter is Coming, 146

G

Galen, 16

Gentile, Giovanni, 154
Green, Joshua, 164
    Devil's Bargain, 164

H

Habermas, Jorge
    A Post-Secular Europe, 6, 8, 42, 82, 85
    Philosophical Discourse on Modernity, 55
Haider, Jörg, 46
Havel, 52
Heidegger, Martin, 68, 69
Held, Kurt, 61
Herberg, Will, 44
Hildegard of Bingen, 79
Homer, 16, 27, 28, 74, 124
Howe, Neil, 109
Humanism, Christian, 13, 17, 18
Huntington, Samuel, 45
    Religious Pluralism, 45, 46
Husserl, Edmund, 49, 50, 53, 67

I

Islamophobia, 3, 11

J

Jesus Christ, 15, 18, 20, 21
John Paul II, 58, 86, 119
Jones, David, 80
Julian of Norwich, 79
Jung, Carl, 28, 30, 94

K

Kasparov, 146
Kierkegaard, Soren, 14
King, Martin Luther, 14

Index

Kjaesgaard, Pia, 2
Koestler, Arthur, 164
   Darkness at Noon, 164

L

Lang, Berel, 72
   Enlightenment Prejudices, 73
   Genocide and Kant's Enlightenment,, 72
Leviathan, 93, 94, 96
   Biblical, 63, 71, 94, 96
   Hobbes, Thomas, 94
Levinas, Emmanuel, 32
   Beyond Essence, 69
   Otherness, 41, 70
   Totality and Infinity, 69
liberation theology, 20
Lucretius, 52
Luther, Martin, 14, 18

M

Machiavelli, Niccolo, 118, 119
Maimonides, 72
Manji, Irshad, vii, 7, 8, 11
   America at a Crossroads, 9
   How to Reconcile Faith and Freedom, 8
   The Trouble with Islam Today, 8
Marcel, Gabriel, 14
Marshal Plan, 135, 136, 138, 139, 140
Marx, Karl, 59, 61
Merton, Thomas, 14
Michelangelo, 18, 79
Mounier, Emmanuel, 14
Mussolini, Benito, 118, 141, 155

N

nationalism, 3, 51, 97, 105, 107, 142, 144, 149, 151

NATO, 120, 131, 133, 134, 136, 143, 146, 148, 149, 150, 156
Newman, John Henry, 14
Niebuhr, Reinhold, 14
Nietzsche, Friedrich, 53, 107

O

O'Connor, 20

P

Pascal, Blaise, 14
Patocka, Jan, 52
Paul, 14, 63, 72, 162, 165
Peguy, Charles, 14
Pew, May, 3
philosophy of religion, 38, 48, 54
Pius X, viii, 117, 118, 120
Pius XIII, viii, 117, 118, 120
Plato, vii, 15, 16, 23, 24, 25, 26, 27, 28, 30, 31, 32, 34, 35, 51, 52, 53, 71, 73, 74, 124, 126, 154, 156, 157
   Myth of the Cave, 26, 27
   Protagoras, 32
   Sophist, 32
   Theaetetus, 32
Pope Francis, viii, 14, 99, 101, 105, 107, 159, 161, 162

R

Raffarin, Jean-Pierre, 47
Rasputin, 164
Reagan, Ronald, 163
Redemptoris Missio, 90
Reuchlin, Johann, 21
Rosenweig, Franz, 73
   Echoes from the Holocaust, 73
Ryan, Paul, 162, 165

S

Sayers, 20
secularism, 5, 6, 8, 40, 42, 47, 89, 140
Solzhenitsyn, Alexander, 20
Sorrentino, Paolo, 118
Spadaro, Antonio, 159, 160
St. Dominick, 79
Strabo, 16
Strauss, William, 109

T

Tillich, Paul, 14
Troeltsch, Ernst, 50, 51
Trump, Donald, 42, 101, 102, 112, 120, 131, 143, 156, 160, 164

U

United Nations, 137

V

Valery, Paul, 63
Vico, Giambattista, v, 31, 75, 110, 125
Virgil, 64

W

Weiler, JHH, 84, 85
   A Christian Europe?, 85
West, Cornell, 9
   Moral Courage, 8, 9
white supremacy, viii, 109, 162
Wiesel, Elie, 69
   Legends of Our Time, 69
Wilberforce, William, 19
Wilders, Geert, 2
Williams, 20
world bank, 135, 136, 138

X

xenophobia, 3, 11, 57, 166